MODERN
AMERICAN
CAPITALISM

MODERN AMERICAN CAPITALISM

Understanding Public Attitudes and Perceptions

Robert A. Peterson,
Gerald Albaum,
and George Kozmetsky

Prepared under the auspices of the IC² Institute

QUORUM BOOKS
New York • Westport, Connecticut • London

Library of Congress Cataloging-in-Publication Data

Peterson, Robert A.
  Modern American capitalism : understanding public attitudes and
perceptions / Robert A. Peterson, Gerald Albaum, and George
Kozmetsky.
      p.   cm.
  "Prepared under the auspices of the IC² Institute."
  Includes bibliographical references and index.
  ISBN 0-89930-625-X (alk. paper)
  1. Capitalism—United States—Public opinion. 2. Public opinion—
United States. I. Albaum, Gerald S. II. Kozmetsky, George.
III. Title.
  HB501.P4156   1990
  330.12'2'0973—dc20   90-42966

British Library Cataloguing in Publication Data is available.

Library of Congress Catalog Card Number: 90-42966
ISBN: 0-89930-625-X

First published in 1990

Quorum Books, 88 Post Road West, Westport, CT 06881
An imprint of Greenwood Publishing Group, Inc.

Printed in the United States of America

The paper used in this book complies with the
Permanent Paper Standard issued by the National
Information Standards Organization (Z39.48-1984).

10 9 8 7 6 5 4 3 2 1

Contents

Figures and Tables

Preface

Thus far during the twentieth century books on capitalism have appeared at the rate of one per week. In The University of Texas at Austin library alone, there are 903 books with the word "capitalism" in their titles and an additional 3,378 books with the word "capital" in their titles. It is obvious (and, at least to us, somewhat surprising) that considerable attention has been accorded capitalism in the literature. Given this attention, the obvious question arises . . . is another book on capitalism necessary? We believe the answer is an unequivocal "yes."

Perusal of the existing inventory of books on capitalism leads to several conclusions. On balance, the literature on capitalism is more negative than positive. Books that offer a negative treatment of capitalism outnumber those offering a positive treatment by a substantial margin. Consider the following (fairly typical) titles of books on capitalism:

- *Capitalism and Slavery*
- *Capitalism and Apartheid*
- *Capitalism and Colonialism*
- *Capitalism and Inequality*
- *Capitalism and Fascism*
- *Capitalism and Morality*
- *Capitalism and the Permissive Society*
- *Capitalism at an Impasse*

As might be expected, the contents generally reflect the implications of the titles.

In brief, there appear to be very few balanced treatments of capitalism. Those that attempt a balance tend to be descriptive in their contents.[1] If not negative, a sizable minority of the books on capitalism tend to be esoteric and pursue certain abstract relationships between capitalism and other phenomena.[2]   Last, many of the books tend to be philosophical and/or political in nature. Frequently the authors offer personalistic visions of capitalism, with their treatments buttressed more by anecdotes and homilies than generalizable data.[3]

Given the existing inventory, the present book fills a notable gap in the literature. The book is unique in that it systematically and formally documents the American public's understanding of, attitudes toward, and perceptions regarding capitalism during the 1980s. The book is, to the best of our knowledge, the first attempt to focus expressly on capitalism through empirical survey research. As such, the book is in the genre of Lipset and Schneider's *The Confidence Gap* and McClosky and Zaller's *The American Ethos* in that all three are concerned with public attitudes and all three rely on survey data.[4]   However, whereas Lipset and Schneider's book is based on secondary data and focuses on attitudes toward the institutions of government, business, and labor, the present book is based on primary data and has as its focus the construct underlying these institutions. And, whereas McClosky and Zaller's work possesses normative overtones and treats capitalism in the context of societal values, our work is limited to providing an empirical perspective on capitalism.

We became interested in our topic in the late 1970s. At that time, we noted an absence of information on what the American public thought about capitalism. While it was possible to *infer* public opinion through studies addressing the American business system, no direct assessment of the public view of capitalism was available.[5]   Consequently, we began to formulate a program of research to document the public's attitudes, understanding, and perceptions. This book is the culmination of that research.

Data for the studies reported in the book were derived from questionnaires administered to more than 10,000 individuals, enough people to populate a city. National samples of the general public, newspaper editors (gatekeepers of the public's information about capitalism), and college students (future societal leaders) were surveyed by telephone or mail interviews and queried about several facets of capitalism.

The research reported in the book covers a decade of empirical investigations conducted at the IC[2] Institute at The University of Texas at Austin. During that decade many significant societal and economic changes took place. In what may, in retrospect, be termed a general industrial restructuring, companies such as Drexel Burnham Lambert went from being virtually unknown to making billion dollar profits and compensating at least one of its executives in excess of $500 million a year, to filing for bankruptcy. Since the functioning and viability of an economy is in part a consequence of the public's acceptance of its underlying ideology, this book carries an important message for social scientists, economists, and business and political leaders (and would-be leaders) in particular, and virtually anyone generally interested in American capitalism.

We are neither "pro-" nor "anti-" capitalism.   Rather, we have attempted to convey, as dispassionately as possible, the American public's view of capitalism during the 1980s.   As such, we hope the book will stimulate discussion of capitalism as well as identify a public mind-set heretofore unknown.

As can be noted from the text, some of the research reported here has previously been published in the academic literature.   The purpose of the book is to coalesce this oftentimes somewhat disparate research and provide a comprehensive portrait of the public's view of capitalism.   Throughout the research, we have employed only standard, accepted research procedures and statistical techniques.   We have attempted to be very conservative in interpreting relationships and differences and in drawing conclusions. Because of the relatively large sample sizes, we have employed statistical significance levels that are relatively small (e.g., .001) as standards rather than the traditional, some might say "sacred cow," significance level of .05. This was done in full cognizance of the intent of our inquiry and to guard against statistical aberrations.   In other words, throughout the research our emphasis has been on substantive relationships or practical differences as opposed to merely focusing attention on relationships or differences found to be "statistically significant."   As a consequence, we are confident that our findings, some of which may be counterintuitive, have meaningful, practical implications.

Finally, it is important to note in passing that our use of footnotes and citations is "mid-range."   Rather than attempting to be exhaustive, we have been purposefully selective in our referencing so as not to overwhelm the reader.   References and citations are used only if they are material to the substance of the discourse.

Many individuals have assisted us in the conduct of the research.   Most important are our families, without whose encouragement and support we would not have been able to complete this work.   In addition to our families, we owe a debt of gratitude to numerous graduate assistants, research associates, and colleagues, of which there are simply too many to thank individually.   Several individuals, however, stand out in terms of their contributions.   Professors Isabella Cunningham and Raymond Smilor were intimately involved in several aspects of the research.   Without the assistance of Nguyen thi Phuong Dung, Catherine Allway, and Galen Bollinger, IC^2 graduate research fellows, and Linda Teague, IC^2 administrative associate, this book would not have been completed.   To these individuals in particular we express our heartfelt gratitude.

NOTES

[1]See, for example, Oliver C. Cox, *Capitalism as a System* (New York: Monthly Review Press, 1964).

[2]An illustration is the dissertation-based book of Dominic Strinati, *Capitalism, the State and Industrial Relations* (London: Croom Helm, 1982).

[3]A prime example is Robert L. Heilbroner's *The Nature and Logic of Capitalism* (New York: W. W. Norton & Company, 1985).

[4]Seymour M. Lipset and William Schneider, *The Confidence Gap* (New York: The Free Press, 1983); Herbert McClosky and John Zaller, *The American Ethos: Public Attitudes toward Capitalism and Democracy* (Cambridge, Massachusetts: Harvard University Press, 1984).

[5]See, for example, Richard B. Wirthlin, "Public Perceptions of the American Business System: 1966-1975," *Journal of Contemporary Business,* Vol. 4 (Summer 1975): 1-14.

MODERN
AMERICAN
CAPITALISM

1

Introduction

As the current and past two decades attest, the economic culture of the United States—its institutions, philosophy and resulting values—is rapidly changing. The 1970s might be characterized as a decade of introspection, whereas the 1980s perhaps represented the start of an age of renewal. Renewal implies awareness of an undesirable *status quo* and a progressive and peaceful correction of conditions that render the *status quo* unappealing.

One consequence of the renewal is that capitalism will be recognized as more than just an economic system. Instead, capitalism will be viewed as an ideology or, as Lodge perceives it, as "a bridge of ideas which a community uses to get values to the real world."[1] In this context, values will simultaneously involve economic, political, and cultural issues and include such concepts as democracy, individualism, equity, and property rights. Consider the commonalities of capitalism and democracy. Michael Novak argues they both breathe vital air from a moral-cultural system based on ideas about the communitarian individual, the social nature of human life, emergent probability, and sin.[2]

This book explores various aspects of *perceptions* of capitalism. For any system to be effective, the public must know what the system involves and be convinced it works well. Does the public have a grasp of the meaning of capitalism and alternative systems? Despite much rhetoric, there has been little empirical research done to measure the American public's perceptions of capitalism and related and alternative constructs.

Because the public ultimately determines the nature of a country's economic system, understanding its perceptions of capitalism is a worthwhile goal. In a democratic and capitalistic society, public awareness is instrumental for both political and economic checks and balances to function efficiently and equitably. Hence the public must, ideally at least, comprehend and appreciate issues of national economic policy if the economic system is to function effectively. Therefore, both public and private sector policymakers must in turn be knowledgeable about public perceptions. The ability to fully comprehend the American economic system transcends the necessity of possessing formal economic education; it does, though, require knowledge of its underlying construct—capitalism.

In this chapter we first discuss ideology and its basis in the United States. Next, we briefly discuss the construct of capitalism, including its underlying dimensions, its evolution, and the nature of attacks being made on it. We conclude the chapter with a brief overview of the materials to follow in the remainder of the book.

THE STATE OF IDEOLOGY[3]

For some time, the United States has been moving from one ideological framework to another. The old structures are disintegrating and newer ones—for better or worse—are replacing them. It is this transition that causes institutions to tremble. Most of the basic institutions (e.g., marriage, family, schools, business, and government) have undergone, and continue to undergo, radical transformation. These institutions and the consequences of their transformation will affect, and be affected by, the collective economic, political, and ethical values of the public, that is, by the prominent ideology of the time.

Any ideology can be viewed as consisting of five basic components:

- The individual human being, his or her rights and place in society, the definition of the individual's fulfillment and self-respect, and the means by which these are to be achieved.
- The means by which individual rights are to be guaranteed.
- The mechanisms and criteria for controlling the exploitation of material resources.
- The role of the state and the function of government.
- The nature and organization of knowledge, particularly the function of science.

The United States derives its ideology primarily from seventeenth-century England, most notably from the views of John Locke. The Lockean ideology is based on five tenets. These tenets are:

- *Individualism.* The community is perceived as no more than the sum of its individuals. The ideas of equality (e.g., equal opportunity) and contract are essential. Individualism and capitalism, although they develop independently, are contingent upon each other.[4]

- *Property rights.* Individual rights are best guaranteed by the sanctity of property rights.
- *Competition.* As Adam Smith argued, the uses of property are thought to be best controlled by each entity competing in an open market to satisfy individual consumer desires.
- *The limited state.* The least government is deemed to be the best government. Preference is for government to *respond* to crises and interest groups rather than to engage in planning.
- *Scientific specialization and fragmentation.* A widely endorsed notion is that if experts and specialists attend to the parts, the whole will take care of itself.

In contrast to Lockean ideology, Lodge suggests American ideology consists of different elements (see below).[5] He posits a model that links values to the real world through ideology. Ideology is influenced by both values and the real world, but influences only the real world. In Lodge's model, Lockean individualism is being augmented and replaced by *communitarianism,* where the community is more than just the sum of its individuals. A vital aspect of communitarianism is cooperation, which Johnson defines as the basic phenomenon distinguishing the human species from subhuman species.[6] He believes cooperation is the underpinning of everything, including socialism and capitalism, business and family. Any society, even one obsessed with competition, is predicated on, and requires, some degree of cooperation.

Elements of . . .

Locke Ideology	Lodge Ideology
1. Individualism	1. Communitarianism
2. Property rights	2. Rights of membership
3. Competition	3. Community need
4. The limited state	4. State as planner
5. Scientific specialization and fragmentation	5. Holism

Second, *rights of membership* are augmenting and replacing Lockean property rights, reducing the distinction between owning and renting property. Of more importance is the ability to enjoy the use of property. Further, property rights seem to have been superseded in political and social importance by the right to survive, to enjoy income, health, and other rights associated with membership in the community known as the United States of America.

The method for controlling the use of property is also changing. *Community need* appears to be replacing the criterion of unfettered competition. The role of government has changed drastically. The concept of *state as planner* has emerged and taken hold. Government is becoming an arbiter of community needs, increasingly taking on tasks of coordination, priority setting, and planning. It is making more and more decisions regarding the trade-offs confronting society. With more and more frequency, a blending of the role of government and community needs, rather than competition, determines how property is used. For example, in 1986 the United States Department of Commerce convened a meeting of more than one dozen U. S. semiconductor companies. The purpose of this meeting was to discuss the possibilities of the companies working together to meet the increasing competition of Japanese companies. The final result of this government encouragement was the formation of SEMATECH, a consortium designed to lead the United States back into semiconductor leadership in the international marketplace. Through such mechanisms the U. S. government is supporting technology by actively and directly fostering industrial innovation.[7]

How the roles of competition and government have changed can be seen also by observing the shift in American ideology from the principle of *equity* to *equality*. For example, the Social Security System was developed to inject equity into the economy by safeguarding the aged against the rigors of competition in the event of disaster. Today, after several political changes, this safeguard is used to redistribute income by giving all workers an equal (and fairly high) pension at a cost that increasingly discriminates against higher paid employees. The minimum wage, which keeps rising, similarly epitomizes a movement toward equality that does not necessarily accord with equity. The Robinson-Patman Act, which prohibits quantity discounts that cannot be cost-justified but does not require discounts on large sales that can be cost-justified, is another example.

In contrast to the principle of equality which so often motivates government action, the principle of *efficiency* motivates business firms. A firm makes investments to increase its efficiency. People are employed, transferred, or terminated on the basis of how much they are believed to contribute to the efficiency of the firm. Funds are invested in research that will lead to products or product changes contributing more to firm revenues than to costs. In brief, business decisions, within the limits of human fallibility, are made to improve efficiency. The principle of efficiency has produced an economy that is and has been the most productive in the history of the world. The driving motive is profit from efficiency, and the more competitive the environment, the more vigorously the principle is adhered to.

The final element in Lodge's view of ideology is *holism*. A prevalent concept among business and community organizations is derived from the notion that nature tends to group units of things into wholes, and ultimately into a single, great integrated whole. Thus, a system is itself as important as its parts. Consequently, specialization has given way to a consciousness that all things are interrelated.

Any ideology is, of course, a collection of ideas or principles subject to continuing refinement and change. Such change does not necessarily occur quickly. Rather, it may take years, decades, and even generations for such changes to become a viable force in a society's ideology.

THE CONSTRUCT OF CAPITALISM

The construct of capitalism has been shaped by numerous individuals, often for the sake of different arguments or purposes. In both the academic and popular literature, the word "capitalism" is used often without definition or any distinction as to its dimensions and usually with minimal attention to how the term is perceived or used by the general public. Consider the view of Copeland:

> The word *capitalism* has been assigned a variety of meanings by different writers. Presumably it characterizes broadly both the type of economic organization we have in the United States today and the type that prevailed immediately before the industrial revolution, and has special reference to an aspect common to our pre- and post-industrial revolution types of organization that has significantly to do with capital in some sense.[8]

In this regard, it appears that capitalism suffers from an *identity crisis,* in that it may have come to mean whatever a person wants it to mean.

Other constructs, such as free or private enterprise, and American enterprise, which are often perceived as synonyms of the American capitalistic system, have not been affected by such an identity crisis. Dictionary and literature definitions of free and private enterprise have remained relatively consistent over time. Interestingly, they are an integral part of "American capitalism" when used to circumscribe its complex of institutions, values, and culture.

What are the reasons for such variance in the meaning of one of the major constructs underlying American society? Why is it that other terms closely related to capitalism are apparently better or more widely understood? One of the reasons may be the complexity of the construct. As will be discussed, capitalism is a polemic and abstract term whose meaning encompasses a type of holistic system—a system that has been evolving over time.

Partly because of this complexity, alternative words have been coined to portray significant changes or describe particular attributes within the system. Corporate capitalism, monopoly capitalism, financial capitalism, and security capitalism are but a few of the terms that have been used in attempts to precisely identify various aspects of capitalism. However, rather than clarify the meaning of capitalism, such "derivative" terms only have served to enhance misunderstanding and confusion. A second possible reason for misunderstanding and confusion is that capitalism seems to be associated with "big business," whereas free or private enterprise is associated with, if not small, smaller businesses. Since opinions toward big business are frequently more varied and emotional than those toward small businesses, they add to the misunderstanding of capitalism by increasing its connotations.

Dimensions of Capitalism

Traditionally the term "capitalism" has referred to a set of economic arrangements that are part of a larger system. In the United States, capitalism appears to be inextricably linked to the attributes of an advanced industrial civilization, one with a highly dynamic class system, political democracy, and certain cultural patterns (e.g., individualism).[9] Although linked to such phenomena, capitalism first and foremost connotes a particular type of economic system. Simultaneously, other systems shape and direct both the specific form and expression of capitalism.

More than a decade ago, Bork defined capitalism as "not merely an economic system but a complex of institutions and attitudes, a culture."[10] Going one step further, Novak argued that capitalism is in reality three systems—an economic system, a political system, and a moral-cultural system—that are interdependent to the extent that changes in one simultaneously change the others:

> There are, indeed, three ways to destroy our system. (1) One can destroy its economic genius. (2) One can destroy its political genius. (3) One can destroy its cultural genius. To attack any of these is to attack the other two. Too foolishly do some believe that changes in any one of these will leave the others sound.[11]

Indeed, as Novak points out, economic systems depend on moral-cultural systems.[12] When certain attitudes, habits, beliefs, and aspirations do not exist, economic development is not likely to occur. Yet, even when societies lack resources, strong moral-cultural traditions may facilitate economic development. At the same time, however, the economic system may impose certain demands on the moral-cultural system. Beliefs, morals, customs, and so forth may need to be changed if development is to occur.

Other systems—religion and education come immediately to mind—also influence the form and expression of capitalism. However, to the extent these institutions do influence capitalism, the influence is indirect through influencing individuals who, in turn, assert their own influence through the political, economic, or moral-cultural systems.

The interrelationship among the economic, political, and moral-cultural systems is one of the major distinctions between capitalism and socialism. Socialism blends the economic system and the political system into one, under the aegis of a single, collective moral-cultural system that can then be interpreted as a comprehensive view of human society.[13] The viability of such a relationship has been described by Kristol, who observed that

> capitalism or a predominantly market economy does seem to be a necessary if not sufficient condition for a liberal-democratic polity. There is no regime in the world, and there never has been a regime, which was liberal-democratic and did not have a predominantly market-oriented economy. One can have the market economy without liberalism or democracy, but one cannot have a liberal democracy without the market economy.[14]

It is important to recognize that economic systems do not exist in a vacuum. Rather, they exist as part of some larger system that includes "social and political structures, cultural patterns, and, indeed, structures of consciousness (values, ideas, belief systems)."[15] Capitalism is no exception; it must be viewed and studied in a societal context.

Several theorists have developed frameworks when attempting to understand the relationship between capitalism and society. Most notable have been Weber, Schumpeter, Hayek, and Marx. Their attempts have resulted in what can be termed middle-range theories. That is, the theories do not purport to be comprehensive. To illustrate, the explanations offered to justify capitalism have been categorized by Kristol as

- *The Protestant Ethic Explanation.* This explanation is based on the premise that worldly success depends on personal virtues such as diligence, (honest) ambition, sobriety, and so on.

- *The Darwinian Ethic Explanation.* This explanation is to be found mainly among small business people who like to think their success is due to "the survival of the fittest."

- *The Technocratic Ethic Explanation.* This is currently the most prevalent explanation for the existence of corporate capitalism; it is based on an advocacy of *performance* as a criterion for success.[16]

The most ambitious effort to achieve an integrated theory that explains capitalism is due to Marx.[17] Closely related is the so-called *modernization theory,* which consists of a set of theoretical efforts presented since the Second World War to explain the rapid changes undergone by the developing (i.e., Third World) societies of Asia, Africa, and Latin America.[18]

There are many who believe these theoretical efforts cannot be supported empirically, and consequently these efforts are misdirected and nonproductive. In fact, many constructs offered in the theories are not capable of being empirically tested and are therefore not subject to falsification.

One recent attempt to integrate the economic, social, political, and cultural dimensions of capitalism into a single theoretical construct is the work of the sociologist Berger.[19] A major premise of his research is that capitalism is an economic system, and a key concept is *economic culture,* which can be interpreted to mean for the economic dimension what "political culture" means to political science. An economic culture theory of capitalism focuses on the social, political, and cultural context within which economic processes operate. Thus, an economic culture contains a number of elements crafted into a totality. No a priori assumptions are made about causality, especially directional relationships. Rather, causal relations are left to empirical inquiry.

Berger has offered fifty propositions—hypotheses subject to empirical testing. As hypotheses, these propositions are capable of falsification. Carrying out such empirical tests would enable observers of capitalism to be able to determine those elements that are intrinsically linked (i.e., those that cannot occur without the others) and those that are extrinsically linked (i.e., an historical accident or something that can be "thought away" from the phenomenon).

Interestingly, Berger has proposed a number of propositions about East Asia.[20] He argues that capitalism in East Asia is different from that in the West in that East Asia has created a new model of industrial capitalism. Of special note is capitalism development in Japan and the so-called Four Little Dragons: Hong Kong, Taiwan, South Korea, and Singapore. Because these societies have evolved with features different from those of Western-based capitalism, the East Asian model cannot necessarily be transposed successfully to other parts of the world. Moreover, the East Asian model probably cannot even be transposed to the People's Republic of China (PRC) as the latter evolves more and more toward its own formulation of capitalism. To an extent, the East Asian model may very well be adopted in the PRC when Hong Kong becomes part of China in 1997. This depends on whether the leaders of China follow through on their promise to allow Hong Kong to operate much as it does prior to reversion. The events of mid-1989, when the old-line conservatives solidified their power in the PRC might suggest, however, that such a promise may not be kept.

The reason for briefly discussing selected theoretical frameworks has not been to refute or advocate one theory or another. Rather, the purposely oversimplified discussion was to provide a context and perspective for the research to be reported. Even so, however, we recognize and advocate the need for a unified, testable theory of capitalism. This position will become clearer as the book progresses.

EVOLUTION OF CAPITALISM AS A CONSTRUCT

Investigation of the evolution of the term "capitalism" and the construct it represents reveals insights regarding the variety of meanings currently ascribed to it. The French historian Braudel provided one of the most useful perspectives on the term's etymology by examining the emergence of the terms "capital," "capitalist," and "capitalism."[21]

The Latin word *capitale* emerged in the twelfth to thirteenth centuries and initially was loosely defined. It gradually came to mean money capital of a firm or a merchant. A cluster of rival terms, including goods, assets, and even patrimony, developed around it over the next two centuries. By the sixteenth century, capital was becoming identified with the wealth of a nation. In the nineteenth century, Marx popularized the word and defined it explicitly and exclusively as "means of production."

The term "capitalist" appeared in the mid-seventeenth century to describe the rich: "Men of means, millionaires, *nouveau riches,* moneybags, *fortunes.*" By the eighteenth century, it was used to describe possessors of "public lands, of stocks and shares, or liquid money for investing." The term has never had a positive connotation, nor has it implied investor or entrepreneur. It has remained attached to the idea of money or wealth for its own sake.

"Capitalism" is a recent term. Not until the beginning of the twentieth century did the term appear in political debate as the natural opposite of socialism. Although Marx never used the exact term, the notion of capitalism was incorporated into his theoretical model of society. Consequently, it became a word with political connotations. It has, according to Braudel, acquired a plethora of meanings and definitions. Yet, no better term has emerged to take its place.

Gras, among others, has traced the historical evolution of capitalism.[22] In so doing, he described seven different phases through which capitalism—as an economic system—has progressed. These phases are summarized in Table 1.1. According to Gras, capitalism in the United States did not start until the second phase. Using his conceptual model, the United States is currently in the phase of security capitalism. However, there are examples of capitalists that have survived from earlier phases. Most notable perhaps are those companies and industries practicing what is essentially industrial capitalism or mature industrial capitalism.

Capitalism under Attack

Perusal of a wide variety of media reveals capitalism has been under siege for nearly half a century. Those who favor capitalism are concerned for its future. For example, Jones noted the "conventional wisdom" that

> The capitalistic system is already declining in importance and will inevitably be replaced by an alternative economic arrangement, probably some form of socialism.[23]

Other writers express the view that the panacea for the problems of American society rests in a new social order and a different economic system.[24] Despite often virulent attacks, capitalism remains resilient, although perhaps not in a form that one would expect from a standard dictionary definition. Moreover, its demise does not appear imminent.

A cornerstone of capitalism is the concept of a *free market*. How such a market is supposed to work has been discussed by Simon:

> Day in and day out, people engage in economic activities called businesses. . . .They organize and allocate resources by selling and buying in markets which respond sensitively to the wishes of individuals. Each consumer "votes," in effect, with his dollar in untold thousands of market "elections," and his vote is automatically translated into shifts of resources into the desired products and services. The products for which people are willing to pay an adequate price are produced; things for which people are not willing to pay an adequate price are not produced.
>
> The free market is nothing but the sum of these interacting individual decisions. It is the most individualistic and the most democratic economic system conceivable.
>
> It works with no conscious direction [or supervision]. There is no single purpose or goal. Each "voter" has his own purposes and goals; he seeks to maximize his rewards, to avoid or to cut his losses.[25]

Table 1.1   Phases of American Capitalism

Petty Capitalism: not treated, because American business began during mercantile capitalism.*

Mercantile Capitalism: up to 1815, sedentary merchant with multiple functions—eventually overspecialization.

Industrial Capitalism: 1815-1866, one-industry management, extreme competition, power machinery in manufacturing and transportation—eventually overspecialization and overcompetition.

Mature Industrial Capitalism: 1866-1933, successful industrial capitalists diversified products, integrated functions, created financial reserves, dispersed plants through merger or otherwise.

Financial Capitalism: 1893-1933 ("duality of capitalism"), less successful industrial capitalists and mature industrial capitalists turned to bankers for help and direction. Methods of operation included the following: build reserves, appoint able executive, purchase of competitors or mergers, policy of diversification and integration, interlocking directorates, trusts for five to ten years, and nonvoting stock.

National Capitalism: 1933-1953, political control of private capital, regulation of financial capitalists and speculations, taxation, assistance to those neglected by financial capitalists, employment, government ownership of utilities, The New Deal, overregulation.

Security Capitalism: 1953-   , shift from government policymakers back to businessmen with more social responsibility toward the "rank and file." Economic security through institutionalizing relief. Dangers to security capitalism include war, government bankruptcy, consumer credit, depression or recession, and socialistic measures.

Source: Adapted from Norman S. B. Gras, *op. cit.*, p. 442.

*A discussion of petty capitalism can be found in Norman S. B. Gras, *Business and Capitalism* (New York: F. S. Crofts, 1939).

Casual observation indicates that the economic systems of many countries purporting to follow capitalism do not exhibit such "ideal" behavior. These countries might be more properly described as having *modified* free markets.

While an issue of semantics may be involved here, it is clear to observers of the American economic system that capitalism has been changing, primarily in response to government intervention. It is interesting that some of the actions taken by the Reagan Administration (1981-1988) were attempts to direct the economic system back toward the classical meaning of capitalism, whereas actions of the Congress appeared in some cases to be moving toward fulfilling the exhortations of system critics. To illustrate what happens when capitalism is not allowed to work to its fullest potential, consider what many have called the economic crisis of the United States in the 1980s—the loss of competitive advantage. In many cases United States companies did not keep up in developing new technology and products. Consequently, competitive advantages in domestic and foreign markets were lost. Some observers believe that this, and other phenomena which have adversely affected the economy, resulted from both government activity and inactivity. In their view, the government was guilty of overregulating businesses, interfering in the marketplace, following inappropriate monetary and fiscal policies, pursuing conflicting and inconsistent policies, and assigning higher priorities to social policy areas other than the economy.[26] As we have indicated earlier, there are efforts on the part of government to help business in some industries, particularly the high technology ones, reverse the process and increase competitive advantages. In addition, companies themselves are taking corrective action without direct government help.[27]

The trend is clear—capitalism will continue to be under attack. Survival depends on understanding how capitalism works, why it is being attacked, and by whom. Bork raised the following rather alarming prospects for capitalism when he stated that the United States is

> moving with worrisome rapidity toward a condition in which the term capitalism will not be appropriate. . . there is not much attachment to the capitalist system and. . . there is indeed a good deal of antipathy toward it.
>
> The causes of this hostility are not easy to describe. In America there is no serious political movement that demands the abolition of capitalism as such, and yet capitalism is weaker than when such movements existed. Though there is widespread irritation with the costs and meddlesomeness of government, the polls show that the same people want more programs from government. The public generally appears not to understand that it is the attempt to fulfill its own demands that angers it.
>
> But it is the intellectual classes and particularly their academic centers that pose the greatest threat to the survival of capitalism. (By the "intellectual classes," I mean the large, interconnected groups which make their livings working with ideas, people who are primarily verbalists: academics, journalists, lawyers, government staffs, etc. To be a member of an intellectual class, one need not be intellectually distinguished or even competent. Membership is defined by the

nature of one's work, and it is characterized by distinctive interests and attitudes.)[28]

Opponents of capitalism have five general classes of criticism. They believe capitalism fosters:

- inequality within a society.
- inequality between societies.
- political oppression.
- ecological dangers.
- a dehumanizing effect due to emphasis on materialism and the existence of greed.[29]

Many of these charges seem to come from intellectuals and the newly emerging "knowledge class." These individuals appear to oppose capitalism on the grounds that vulgar merchants, not intellectuals, have been accorded an elevated status by capitalism.[30]

More generally, opponents have criticized capitalism as not fulfilling its implied promises.[31] Capitalism allegedly promised continued improvement in the material conditions of all its citizens, an unprecedented measure of freedom for these citizens, and prosperity and liberty that would allow the individual to satisfy his or her instinct to lead a virtuous life; the free exercise of individual virtue would aggregate into a just society. Apparently it is the voiced failure of capitalism to deliver completely on the latter—a virtuous life and a just society—that has given fuel to critics. At least that seems to be the position taken by the Catholic church in the United States to the extent it believes capitalism has failed to meet the needs of the poor.[32]

In spite of such attacks, there is a lack of empirical evidence regarding how the general populace views capitalism, although inferences can be made from polls assessing public opinion toward business and other societal institutions. According to these polls, public confidence and trust in business has been eroding for many years, and there is a belief that business has too much influence in society. Careful inspection of the poll findings, though, suggests loss of confidence has been general and has affected every major societal institution, although certainly some have been more affected than others. To illustrate, Figure 1.1 contains results from surveys conducted by the National Opinion Research Center. In these surveys respondents are asked to indicate the extent of confidence ("a great deal," "only some," or "hardly any") they have in the people running selected institutions in the United States. As can be seen, public confidence in both military and business leaders has declined across all age groups. In particular, business, labor, and government leaders seem to possess the least confidence of the general public and appear to be the most distrusted because they are

Figure 1.1   Percentage of Public Indicating a Great Deal of Confidence in Leaders in 1970s and 1980s by Age

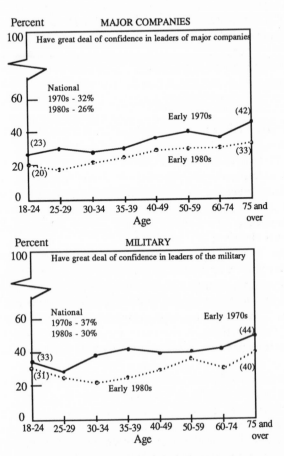

Note: For the 1970s data are combined for the years 1973 and 1974, whereas for the 1980s data for 1980, 1982, and 1983 are combined.

Source: Reported in *Public Opinion*, Vol. 6 (December/January 1984): 32.

perceived primarily to be motivated by self-interest.[33] Indeed, according to Duggan, there has emerged in the United States an *adversary culture* that has led to the existence of a sullen and skeptical populace, literally demoralized in its attitude toward its leaders and its major institutions.[34]

    Although the public has reported losing much of its faith in business, this loss should be interpreted in the context of the major companies and the people who manage these companies. There is resentment of *big* business, and concentration of power in the hands of the self-interested is viewed as inherently dangerous and untrustworthy. One must not confuse, however, a system with the individual elements that constitute the system. The public does not appear to be ready to abandon capitalism itself. Anecdotal and indirect evidence suggest that, contrary to what appears in the media and the criticism of opponents of capitalism, the general public perceives capitalism quite favorably.

PREVIEW OF THE BOOK

Prior to understanding the public's perception of capitalism, it is necessary to understand what capitalism is, and what it is not. Thus, the next chapter explores several definitions of capitalism. Also presented are results of a content analysis of a sampling of definitions. Chapter 2 concludes by presenting the results of a survey ascertaining the extent to which the general public correctly defines capitalism.

Chapter 3 examines attitudes toward capitalism as revealed by a nationwide survey. A representative sample of the general public was asked to respond to a series of attitude statements about capitalism. In addition to determining the attitudes of the general public, the survey investigated relationships between demographic characteristics and attitudes toward capitalism. For comparison purposes, results of studies delving into the attitudes of newspaper editors and "future leaders" (college students) are also reported.

Chapter 4 investigates perceptions of constructs frequently treated as synonymous with capitalism (private enterprise, free enterprise, and American enterprise) as well as constructs considered alternatives to capitalism (socialism and communism). It also examines the perceptual link between business and capitalism and perceptions regarding the relationship between capitalism and size of business firm (small or large).

Chapter 5 reports the results of studies monitoring capitalism attitudes over time. These results serve as a foundation for predicting future attitudes toward capitalism.

Chapter 6 summarizes major study findings and discusses their implications. It also offers suggestions for measuring and monitoring perceptions and knowledge of capitalism in the future.

NOTES

[1]George C. Lodge, "The Large Corporation and the New American Ideology," in *Corporations and the Common Good,* ed. Robert B. Dickie and

Leroy S. Rouner (Notre Dame, Indiana: University of Notre Dame Press, 1986), p. 62.

[2]Michael Novak, "The Judeo-Christian Values that Characterize Economic Freedoms," in *The Future of Private Enterprise*, Vol. 1, ed. Craig E. Aronoff and John L. Ward (Atlanta, Georgia: Georgia State University Press, 1984), p. 26.

[3]This section draws heavily upon material contained in George C. Lodge, *The New American Ideology* (New York: Alfred A. Knopf, 1976), pp. 9-21.

[4]For a thorough treatise on the relationship between individualism and capitalism, see Nicholas Abercrombie, Stephan Hill, and Bryan S. Turner, *Sovereign Individuals of Capitalism* (London: Allen & Unwin, 1986).

[5]Lodge, pp. 17-20.

[6]Cited in Alfie Cohen, "It's Hard to Get Left Out of a Pair," *Psychology Today*, Vol. 21 (October 1987): 52-57.

[7]Cited in John Cory, "Washington, Inc.?" *Business Week,* No. 3110 (June 19, 1989): 40-41.

[8]Morris Copeland, *Our Free Enterprise Economy* (New York: McMillan Company, 1965), p. 78.

[9]Peter L. Berger, *The Capitalist Revolution: Fifty Propositions about Prosperity, Equality, and Liberty* (New York: Basic Books, 1986), p. 16.

[10]Robert H. Bork, "Will Capitalism Survive?" *Yale Alumni Magazine and Journal*, Vol. 61 (April 1978): 15-17.

[11]Michael Novak, "An Underpraised and Undervalued System," in *The Moral Basis of Democratic Capitalism* (Washington, DC: American Enterprise Institute, Reprint No. 115, 1980), p. 32.

[12]See Michael Novak, "The Judeo-Christian Values That Characterize Economic Freedoms," pp. 5-30

[13]Michael Novak, "The Vision of Democratic Capitalism," *Public Opinion*, Vol. 4 (April/May 1982): 7.

[14]Irving Kristol, "Capitalism Versus Anticapitalism: The Moral and Political Issues," in *Private Enterprise and the New Global Economic Challenge,* ed. Stephen Guisinger (Indianapolis: Bobbs-Merrill Educational Publishing, 1979), p. 40.

[15]Berger, p. 24.

[16]Irving Kristol, *Two Cheers for Capitalism* (New York: Basic Books, 1978), pp. 263-264.

[17]A good source for an overview of the intellectual efforts of Marx is Leszek Kolakowski, *Main Currents of Marxism* (Oxford: Clarendon Press, 1978).

[18]For a useful overview of these efforts see Myron Weiner ed., *Modernization: The Dynamics of Growth* (New York: Basic Books, 1966).

[19]Berger, *The Capitalist Revolution*.

[20]Berger, Chapter 7.

[21]See Fernand Braudel, *Civilization and Capitalism: 15th-18th Century,* Vol. 2, *The Wheels of Commerce* (New York: Harper & Row, 1981), pp. 221-239.

[22]Norman S. B. Gras, *Business History of the United States* (Ann Arbor, Michigan: Edward Brothers, 1967).

[23]Sidney L. Jones, "Free Enterprise: Its Survival Is Up to You," *Business,* Vol. 30 (July/August 1980): 13.

[24]See Oliver C. Cox, *Capitalism as a System* (New York: Monthly Review Press, 1964); Michael Harrington, *The Twilight of Capitalism* (New York: Simon and Schuster, 1976); and Michael Kidron, *Capitalism and Theory* (New York: Pluto Press, 1974).

[25]William E. Simon, *A Time for Truth* (New York: Reader's Digest Press, 1978), p. 23.

[26]Terry F. Russ, F. Stevens Redburn and Larry C. Ledelus, "The Economic Revitalization of America: An Overview of the Issues," *Policy Studies Review,* Vol. 1 (May 1982): 750.

[27]See various articles in the June 16, 1989 issue of *Business Week.*

[28]Bork, pp. 15, 16.

[29]Peter Berger, "The Moral Crisis of Capitalism," in *Corporations and the Common Good,* ed. Robert B. Dickie and Leroy S. Rouner, pp. 19-24. Also see R. Nolan and F. Kirkpatrick, *Living Issues in Ethics* (Belmont, California: Wadsworth Publishing, 1982), pp. 259-267.

[30]Berger, "The Moral Crisis of Capitalism," p. 25, and Robert Nozick, "Why Do Intellectuals Oppose Capitalism?" in *The Future of Private Enterprise,* Vol. 3, ed. C. Aronoff, R. Goodwin, and J. Ward, (Atlanta, Georgia: Georgia State University Press, 1986), pp. 133-143.

[31]See I. Kristol, *Two Cheers for Capitalism,* pp. 257-259.

[32]See "The Church and Capitalism," *Business Week,* No. 2868 (November 12, 1984): 104-112, and George Dennis O'Brien, "The Christian Assault on Capitalism," *Fortune,* Vol. 114 (December 8, 1984): 181, 183.

[33]See, for example, Seymour M. Lipset and William Schneider, "How's Business? What the Public Thinks," *Public Opinion,* Vol. 1 (July/August 1978): 41-47; and A. Lawrence Chickering, "Warming Up the Corporate Image," *Public Opinion,* Vol. 5 (October/November 1982), pp. 13-15.

[34]Erwin S. Duggan, "Save the Whales!" *Public Opinion,* Vol. 6 (April/May 1983): 13.

2

Defining Capitalism

Given the negative perceptions of business the public appears to have, a question arises as to whether capitalism, as a construct, is really understood. Little empirical evidence exists concerning what capitalism means to Americans (or any nationality, for that matter), despite the relatively large amount of rhetoric about it. A related issue is whether the public believes "descriptive" terms such as private, free, or American enterprise are synonymous with capitalism, or whether they are perceived to describe different systems. Additionally, little research has been reported about the public's perceptions of socialism and communism as alternative systems to capitalism.

The present chapter discusses various definitions of capitalism. Formal definitions from the literature are initially assessed through content analysis to establish its essence. This is followed by a discussion of empirical research regarding the public's definition of capitalism.

Partly because of capitalism's perceived complexity, and partly because of the emotions it evokes, alternative terms frequently have been coined to emphasize particular facets or describe specific changes over time. Among these terms are "petty capitalism," "financial capitalism," "managerial capitalism," and "national capitalism."[1] (Table 1.1.) Simultaneously, there is a tendency, when discussing the U. S. economic system, to use terms such as free enterprise system, private enterprise system, or American enterprise system instead of capitalism. Because of their widespread use, definitions of these terms were also studied, both as they exist in the literature and in the common vernacular.

Regardless of the term used to describe the construct of capitalism, there must be at least some agreement about its meaning. This is true not only for the intelligentsia, proponents as well as opponents of capitalism, but also for the general public as well. For capitalism, or any alternative construct, to be effectively discussed at the policy level, how it is perceived by the public must be ascertained and understood. The ability to comprehend, participate in, and make informed judgments about the American economic system requires an understanding of capitalism.

FORMAL DEFINITION

Capitalism has long been a troubling and quarrelsome word, in part because of the emotion-laden images it conjures up. Throughout history the meaning of capitalism has been controversial and at times even contradictory. Consequently, it is frequently applied indiscriminately, and usually pejoratively, to support or refute a particular political or philosophical position.

Contrary to popular belief, Adam Smith never used the word "capitalism" in his classic *Wealth of Nations*. Rather, its meaning was derived from and popularized by proponents of Marxian viewpoints, who applied it to describe the antithesis of utopian socialism. Moreover, modern-day economists rarely use the term, preferring instead the term "private ownership economy."[2]

Capitalism has been defined in a number of different ways. Table 2.1 presents illustrative definitions from dictionary and other literary sources. Although a limited sample, these definitions suggest three conclusions. First, there is little agreement as to what capitalism actually is. Second, common attributes ascribed to capitalism by the definitions include ownership (private or corporate), production, private enterprise and decisions, free market and competition, and concentration, accumulation, and reinvestment. Third, there appears to be a broadening of its meaning; the most recent formal definitions identify capitalism as being not only an economic system, but also a political and social system. This broader view is consistent with the perspective in Chapter 1 that capitalism is part of a complex of institutions and attitudes that collectively constitute a culture.[3]

DIMENSIONS OF CAPITALISM

To better circumscribe capitalism as a construct, a content analysis of approximately one hundred definitions of capitalism was undertaken. These definitions were found through a representative sampling of dictionaries, economic and philosophical treatises, political and sociological monographs, and essays that collectively reflect an eclectic whole commonly referred to as a written body of knowledge relating to capitalism. Repetitive definitions were not included, therefore limiting the content analysis to the qualitative and descriptive content of distinctive definitions of capitalism found.

Table 2.1   Illustrative Definitions of Capitalism

Dictionary Definitions:
An economic system in which capital and capitalists play the principal part; specifically, the system of modern countries in which the ownership of land and natural wealth, the production, distribution, and the exchange of goods and the operation of the system itself are affected by private enterprise and control under competitive conditions.*

An economic system characterized by private or corporation ownership of capital goods, by investments that are determined by private decision rather than by state control, and by prices, production, and the distribution of goods that are determined mainly in a free market.+

(1) An economic system characterized by freedom of the market with increasing concentration of private and corporate ownership of production and distribution means, proportionate to increasing accumulation and reinvestment of profits. (2) A political or social system regarded as being based on this.‡

Literature Definitions:
An economic system consisting largely of commercial transactions between consenting adults.§

A social system based on the recognition of individual rights, including property rights, in which all property is privately owned. //

Is free enterprise. It tends to promote the accumulation and increased use of capital, and so tends constantly and acceleratively to increase the production of wealth. It is a combination of two institutions, private property and a free market.#

---

* *The Universal Dictionary of the English Language* (London: Rutledge and Keegan Publishers, Ltd., 1932).
+ *Webster's Third New International Dictionary* (Springfield, Massachusetts: G&C Merriam Company, 1981).
‡ *American Heritage Dictionary of the English Language,* College Edition (Boston: Houghton Mifflin, 1982).
§ Irving Kristol, "Capitalism Versus Anticapitalism: The Moral and Political Issues," in *Private Enterprise and the New Global Economic Challenge,* ed. Stephen Guisinger (Indianapolis: Bobbs-Merrill Educational Publishing, 1979), p. 40.
// Ayn Rand, *Capitalism: The Unknown Ideal* (New York: The New American Library, 1967), p. 19.
Henry Hazlitt, "The Future of Capitalism," in *Toward Liberty*, Vol. II (Menlo Park, California: Institute for Humane Studies, 1971), pp. 159-171.

Table 2.2 contains the results of the analysis. Four dimensions were used to describe or define capitalism. The dimensions are *economic, political, social,* and *technological.*

The *economic* dimension contains the largest and most consistent set of terms. It includes elements such as private property and ownership, competition, and free enterprise. The *political* dimension includes elements such as freedom, lack of coercion, voluntary, and checks and balances. The *social* dimension includes the elements dynamic, natural laws, and independence. Elements of the *technological* dimension include innovation, invention, efficiency, quality in production, and cost reduction.

From the content analysis, the meaning of capitalism appears to reflect social, ethical, political, and economic values unique to the American culture. This means that capitalism can be understood only within its cultural context. Consequently, the specific dimensions of capitalism covered cannot be transposed to other capitalistic systems in the world. The existence of different cultural contexts increases the difficulty of defining capitalism comprehensively. Cultural aspects have to be understood within the context of a nation's value system. Hence, a universal definition of capitalism—one applicable to all nations and cultures—is unlikely and, indeed, probably should not be sought.

The origin and sources of the four dimensions of capitalism are difficult and perhaps impossible to trace historically. Moreover, the complexity of each dimension makes it difficult to coalesce them into a single coherent definition. Hence, one is left with a feeling of definitional inadequacy when searching for an appropriate, comprehensive description of the construct.

For comparative purposes, content analyses of the literature were conducted on definitions of free enterprise, private enterprise, American enterprise, socialism, and communism. To facilitate interpretation of these constructs, the same dimensions used to describe capitalism were employed as the analytical framework. The results of the analyses are respectively presented in Tables 2.3 through 2.7. Using the four dimensions—economic, political, social, and technological—comparison of capitalism with free, private, and American enterprise reveals a common core of attributes, as there should be. There are some differences, however, as there are differences between the dimensions of the two systems that are sometimes offered as replacements for capitalism. For example, within the realm of the economic dimension, attributes such as private business ownership, private property, market forces, and pursuit of profit emerged for free enterprise, private enterprise, and American enterprise, but not for socialism or communism. For the political dimension, free enterprise and private enterprise have the most similar attributes, including the absence of any government control or ownership of economic enterprises. Socialism and communism fall on the other end of the government ownership and

Table 2.2 Key Dimensions of Capitalism

Economic	Political	Social	Technological
Market economy	Freedom	Ethics	Specialization of labor
Private property in the instruments of production including land	Lack of coercion	Values	Innovation
Private ownership of business	Voluntary	Natural laws	Invention
	Justice	Dynamic	Efficiency
Private decision-making	Checks/balances	"Meeting obligations when due"	Quality in production
Self-regulation	Bankruptcy law	Independence	Cost reduction
Pursuit of profits			
"Surplus values"	Contract law		Patents
Competition in the marketplace			Resource utilization
Free enterprise			
Effective			
Growth			

control spectrum. American enterprise falls somewhere between the two extremes. Parallel similarities and differences emerge for the social and technological dimensions.

How does the American public perceive capitalism? How familiar is it with the "synonyms" of capitalism? In what respects does the American public view capitalism favorably or unfavorably relative to socialism and communism? And what do these perceptions portend for the future of American capitalism? Answers to these and similar questions are presented in the remaining chapters of this book.

Table 2.3   Key Dimensions of Free Enterprise

Economic	Political	Social	Technological
Private business ownership	Absence of government control	Legislation protects individuals, not society	Efficient production
Private property			Good resource utilization
Market forces	Subject only to social conventions	Personal ethics and moral standards prevail	
Pursuit of profits and wealth by individuals			Good for innovations/ inventions
Pure competition	Producers/ consumers free to reach independent market decisions	Individualistic philosophy	Stimulates technology
Very efficient - minimum cost		No social obligations to be met	Good quality products
Competitive entry only	Invisible hand of market forces only control	Firm's responsibility to employees and owners	Cost reductions
Freedom to engage in *any* type of marketing	Firms free to hire, produce, and price as they see fit		
	No monopoly regulations		

THE PUBLIC'S KNOWLEDGE OF CAPITALISM AND RELATED CONSTRUCTS

There are many who have deplored the general economic ignorance of the American public.   The business sector in general, and individual companies specifically, often encounter political problems because the public is not knowledgeable about topics and behaviors such as profits, investments, and inflation.   Understanding such concepts is necessary if there is to be a realistic appraisal of economic policies and political decisions.   Recent research findings suggest that business college students are not well informed when it comes to business-related current events,[4] and the general public is ignorant in everyday economic affairs, particularly regarding broad, overall economic indicators and related phenomena.[5]

Table 2.4   Key Dimensions of Private Enterprise

Economic	Political	Social	Technological
Private business ownership	Government protects private ownership	No interest in social values	Inventions/ innovations spurred
Private property		"Caveat emptor"; firm not	Entrepreneur-
Market forces	No government ownership	responsible for consumer	ship increases technological
Pursuit of profits/ wealth by individuals	Enterprises independently	protection	innovation
Mostly very	managed	Dynamic	Good resource
competitive		Independent	utilization
	No interference		
Very efficient cost	with market	Private	Good quality
reduction	forces	ownership more important	products
Competitive entry	Could allow for concentration of wealth	than social responsibility	Increased emphasis on service/product adaptability

To find out how Americans define capitalism and how they perceive its essence, we conducted a survey among representatives of America's middle class. The remainder of this chapter presents the methodology and results of that survey.[6]

Method

In 1982 a telephone survey was conducted with a randomly selected sample of the general adult population in the continental United States. Using a split-ballot research technique, survey participants were asked to define either *capitalism, free enterprise system, private enterprise system,* or *American enterprise system.* The latter three were selected for investigation since the previously described content analyses of dictionary definitions and literature indicated they had much in common in their meanings and, to a certain extent, could be considered synonymous with capitalism. Initially, the dictionary definition of each construct was decomposed into its major elements to permit detailed comparisons with the survey participants' definitions.

Table 2.5   Key Dimensions of American Enterprise

Economic	Political	Social	Technological
Mixed: both private and government business ownership	Mixed: some government regulation and ownership of production	Social values imposed by regulations	Labor specialization
Private property except where government intervenes	Federal, state, and local regulatory controls	Oligopolies allowed; sometimes regulated	Reduced innovation
Market forces in most industries except where government regulation— utilities, etc.	Large lobbying/ government influence by corporations	Government is society's advocate	Quality of products subject to system's inefficiencies
Pursuit of profits/wealth both by individuals and corporations	Concentration of wealth in hands of corporations	Business has adversary relationship with society	Cost reduction
Competition limited with large corporation control	Professional management vs. individuals	Large corporations set many social values	
Labor unions- inefficiencies	Bureaucratic government		
Entry limited by monopolies and oligopolies			

Interviews were conducted with 1,199 individuals over the age of 18, representing a response rate (in terms of contacts) of 64 percent of the original sample of 1,900. In accordance with the usual application of the split-ballot technique, each individual was questioned about only one of the four constructs, with the specific construct being randomly determined. Specifically, each survey participant was asked the following open-end question: Now, I would like you to briefly define the term [*one of four*]. In your own words please define [*that term*]. Definitions were provided by 888

Table 2.6   Key Dimensions of Socialism

Economic	Political	Social	Technological
Mostly public ownership of productive resources	State distributes wealth to social welfare	No social classes—only employees	Contributes to some growth
No private profit motive	Heavy taxes on property and non-labor income	Redistribution of income to achieve social equality	No planned technological innovation
No market forces	Large-scale government	Large social welfare programs	No production experiences
Planned economy			No major quality
Critical (basic defense) industries owned by the state	Evolutionary to extend ownership and control of production	No motivation to produce	control system
No profit pursuit	No military force to control social efforts	Social needs prevail over individual needs	
Heavy business taxation		"Utopia"	
Restricts private enterprise			

people, or 74 percent of those contacted and 47 percent of the original sample. The distribution of contacts and responses among the sample subgroups are shown in Table 2.8.

Definitions provided by the survey participants were evaluated as to their correctness through a formal content analysis.[7] If a survey participant's definition agreed in principal with one or more of the major elements of the dictionary definition, it was considered correct. If, however, there was a contradiction with at least one of the major elements, a survey participant's definition was considered incorrect.

KNOWLEDGE OF CAPITALISM AND RELATED CONCEPTS

As can be seen from Table 2.8, 73 percent of the individuals queried about capitalism, nearly three out of four, were able to provide an answer.

Table 2.7   Key Dimensions of Communism

Economic	Political	Social	Technological
Public ownership of all resources	Government owns and distributes wealth	Some ownership of consumer goods	Rapid technological growth
Cost efficient		All individual needs are satisfied through government distribution of wealth	Efficient use of resources
Planned economy- no market forces	Military force		
	Dictatorship of proletariat		Planned technological innovation
Production capacity dictates supply			
	Totalitarian, centralized government (in advanced forms — absence of government)	No social classes — only class is proletariat	Quality of product restricted to its utility/use
Need defines consumption			
Only income allowed is through wages			
		Individual produces according to ability and consumes according to need	Individual innovation not allowed

This figure is lower than that for free enterprise system (77 percent) and private enterprise system (81 percent), but higher than that for American enterprise system (64 percent). However, as Table 2.9 shows, less than one-half of the survey participants asked about capitalism and providing an answer were able to define it correctly, whereas more than two-thirds of those responding about the other three constructs were able to define them correctly. This finding is not all that surprising since capitalism encompasses the concepts of free enterprise and private enterprise, and it is not unusual for people to know more about specific components than the whole.

The percentages in column 5 of Table 2.8 and column 1 of Table 2.9 can be combined to yield a single index of *definitional knowledge*. Specifically, of the individuals questioned as to the meaning of the respective constructs investigated,

   35 percent defined capitalism correctly,
   52 percent defined free enterprise system correctly,

Table 2.8   Sample Disposition—Telephone Survey

Construct	Number in Original Sample	Contacts Number	Percent of Original Sample	Respondents Providing Answers Number	Percent of Contacts	Percent of Original Sample
Capitalism	475	300	63.2	219	73.0	46.1
Free enterprise	475	306	64.4	234	77.0	49.2
Private enterprise	475	297	62.5	239	80.5	50.3
American enterprise	475	296	62.3	196	64.4	41.2
Total sample	1,900	1,199	63.1	888	74.0	46.7

59 percent defined private enterprise system correctly, whereas 44 percent defined American enterprise system correctly.

Thus, in general, capitalism was significantly less likely to be defined correctly than were the remaining three constructs.

Table 2.10 reveals how survey participants differed in their definitions. The table shows the percentage of individuals using one or more key definitional terms when responding to the respective constructs. For parsimony, only the sixteen most frequently mentioned terms have been analyzed.

The major terms used when defining capitalism include "one can own his own business" (28 percent response), "money/profit/wealth" (26 percent response), and "free/private enterprise" (21 percent response). Interestingly enough, many survey participants defined capitalism by using terms that are technically incompatible with it, such as "restriction of rights/limited freedom" or "bureaucracy/excessive government." In contrast, individuals defining the other three constructs were much more likely to use terms such as "one can own his own business," "limited government regulation," or "freedom in general."

Moreover, slightly fewer terms were used to define capitalism than were used to define the other three constructs. On average, survey participants used 1.9 terms when defining capitalism as compared with 2.1, 2.0, and 2.1 terms for, respectively, free enterprise system, private

Table 2.9   Knowledge of Four Constructs Describing the American Economic System

| | Percentage of Sample Providing | |
Construct	Correct Definition	Incorrect Definition
Capitalism	47.5	52.5
Free enterprise	67.9	32.1
Private enterprise	72.8	27.2
American enterprise	68.4	31.6
All constructs	64.3	35.7

enterprise system, and American enterprise system.   This implies capitalism evokes fewer associations than the other constructs.

Finally, Table 2.10 suggests there was considerably less agreement as to the meaning of capitalism than there was for the remaining three constructs. On the basis of these results, the general public views capitalism as a more vague, and perhaps even more abstract, construct than the others.

CONCLUSION

Capitalism, at a minimum as it exists in the United States, appears to be suffering from at least two distinct problems. The first is well known: there is continuous pressure to change the American economic system and, consequently, its underlying construct, capitalism. Indeed, there are frequently virulent attacks from a variety of constituencies essentially seeking changes in the manner in which society is organized.[8] The nature of these attacks was discussed in Chapter 1.

In addition, capitalism appears to be suffering from a type of "identity crisis." Capitalism is not well understood by those participating in it.   In fact, it is misunderstood by a sizeable minority.   On the basis of the survey results reported here, only about 35 percent of the American public can correctly define capitalism, a percentage significantly less than that for such related constructs such as private enterprise system, free enterprise system, or American enterprise system. Moreover, capitalism is perceived relatively less positively than two of these constructs.   Only American enterprise

Table 2.10 **Content Analysis of Key Terms Used to Define Constructs Investigated**

| Term | Percentage of Survey Participants Providing Term | | | |
	Capitalism	Free enterprise	Private enterprise	American enterprise
One can own his own business	28.3	63.7	66.9	46.4
Free/private enterprise (explicitly)	21.0	0.9	0.8	16.3
Economic system	6.8	0.9	3.8	3.6
Way U. S. is run economically	3.7	1.3	2.9	4.6
Way U. S. is run politically	12.3	5.6	4.2	10.7
Limited government regulation	11.4	47.9	48.1	32.7
Freedom in general	10.5	24.8	8.4	16.8
Private vs. public ownership	3.7	1.3	7.9	1.5
Laissez faire	3.2	2.6	2.9	5.6
Money/profit/wealth	25.5	11.5	10.5	13.8
Supply and demand	3.7	12.0	5.4	9.7
Competition	2.3	7.3	5.4	4.1
Monopoly/big business	7.3	2.6	7.1	5.1
Concentration of wealth	9.1	0.4	1.7	1.0
Restriction of rights/limited freedom	5.0	---	---	---
Bureaucracy/excessive government	9.1	3.8	2.1	2.0

system possesses negative connotations to the degree that capitalism does. This is discussed in more detail in Chapter 4.

To a certain extent it is not surprising that the public is able to define private enterprise system, free enterprise system, and American enterprise system better than capitalism. Although the three are commonly used as synonyms for capitalism, in fact they are but "parts of the whole" and as such merely circumscribe particular aspects of capitalism. Because capitalism is such a complex construct—it is in fact more than an economic system—it is difficult to define or even adequately capture its essence in any parsimonious fashion. Therefore, the public should not be faulted for failing to properly or precisely define it. Indeed, careful perusal of the voluminous capitalism literature reveals that even well-educated segments of the American public often have at best only a hazy notion of what the construct means.

It is apparent, if only from analysis of the responses obtained in this survey, that capitalism is more than an economic construct with sociological ramifications. Perhaps it is time for a more appropriate definition of capitalism, one that more closely approximates reality as well as specifies its cultural associations and implications. We have offered one possible definition elsewhere: "Capitalism is a dynamic ideology that allows individuals to create and retain wealth through creative endeavors."[9]

The point of this definition is that current definitions of capitalism are inadequate—outmoded and too narrow. They are no longer descriptive of either the American economic system as it exists or what the public wants it to be. Instead, they merely serve as controversy-eliciting stimuli. Consequently, they should be replaced with a more appropriate definition— one based on ideology such as that proffered—and extensive educational programs undertaken to inform the public as to its meaning. Only then will the public be able to effectively participate in discussions that will ultimately lead to a coherent national economic policy.

What could be the reasons for such misunderstanding of one of the basic foundation blocks of our society? Why is it that other concepts closely related to capitalism appear to be better understood? The complexity of the construct itself may be responsible for the confusion about its meaning. It may also be one reason why, as the American economy has developed and changed, alternative words were coined to portray significant changes that have taken place within the economic system. Terms such as corporate capitalism or monopoly capitalism, to just mention only two, could have contributed to the confusion. There is probably some confounding of the term "capitalism" and its modifier (e.g., monopoly, corporate) in the mind of the public. This leads to mixed perceptions and, ultimately, to incorrect definitions. New terms are continually being introduced in our vocabulary to portray changes in our economic system or to emphasize certain characteristics of the system. Often such emphasis is on what a writer believes is a negative characteristic.

Should businesspeople and politicians use the word capitalism? Should other terms such as free enterprise and private enterprise be substituted for it? Economic ignorance does pervade our society, and its influence is likely to affect people's reactions to major economic decisions. This ignorance appears to be widespread; it exists at all levels of education. By using the term capitalism in often contradictory ways, either intentionally or unintentionally, "thought leaders"—intellectuals, media representatives, religious and government leaders, and the like—merely increase confusion and misunderstanding.[10]

There is more to economic ignorance than meets the eye. Those who believe in the traditional capitalistic system and in the values of private and free enterprise as they relate to the American way of life should be aware of the lack of understanding of the American public. Terms such as capitalism that are relatively unfamiliar and misunderstood should be explored fully if the system is to continue to occupy the same place of importance in our culture.

Overcoming such economic ignorance transcends the task of economic education in the formal sense. Those attitudes which may obstruct and discourage knowledge both in the classroom and in society must be changed. Attitudes are lasting and pervasive. They determine behavior, influence political options, and shape socioeconomic values. Attitudes toward capitalism, one of the basic components of our social structure, need not be positive. We are not arguing in *favor* of capitalism or attempting to justify its existence. Instead, we are simply arguing that the American public must be educated as to its meaning so that a common base of understanding exists.

Evidence exists that the public is in favor of formal educational courses that transmit knowledge about the practical and applied aspects of economics. A national survey of nearly 1,500 adults indicated that virtually all of those surveyed, 96 percent, stated that "practical economics courses" should either probably (37 percent) or definitely (59 percent) be offered in the nation's school systems.[11] Of the survey participants stating such courses should be offered, 70 percent believed the courses should be required at the high school level. An additional 16 percent believed they should be offered but not required at the high school level. Given the broad support for economic education courses, it would seem logical to explicitly incorporate a discussion of capitalism in them. Doing so would be a first step toward providing a common base of understanding.

NOTES

[1]Fred L. Fry, "A New Stage of Capitalism," *Business Horizons,* Vol. 21 (April 1978): 23-25.

[2]This term appears to have been used first by Gerard Debreu in *The Theory of Value* (New York: Wiley, 1959), a now-classic book that grew out of a Cowles Foundation monograph and led to Debreu's being awarded the 1983 Nobel Prize in Economics.

[3]Robert H. Bork, "Will Capitalism Survive?" *Yale Alumni Magazine and Journal,* Vol. 61 (April 1978): 15.

[4]Bruce L. Stern, Jack L. Taylor, Jr., Neal Hayden, and Eileen Murphy, "Are Our Students (Il)literate About Business-Related Current Events?" paper presented at the 1985 conference of the Western Marketing Educators' Association.

[5]"Americans' Low Business IQ," *Nations' Business,* Vol. 73 (February 1985): 56.

[6]Most of the remaining material in this chapter has been drawn from Robert A. Peterson, George Kozmetsky, and Gerald Albaum, "On the Public's Perception of Capitalism," *Business Horizons,* Vol. 29 (January/February 1986): 10-14.

[7]See Klaus Krippendorf, *Content Analysis—An Introduction to its Methodology* (Beverly Hills, California: Sage Publications, 1980); Karl

Erik Rosengren, ed., *Advances in Content Analysis* (Beverly Hills, California: Sage Publications, 1981); and Robert Philip Weber, *Basic Content Analysis* (Beverly Hills, California; Sage Publications, 1985).

[8]R. Joseph Monson, "The Future of American Capitalism," *California· Management Review*, Vol. 21 (Spring 1979): 5-16, and Robert Wuthnow, "The Moral Crisis in American Capitalism," *Harvard Business Review,* Vol. 60 (March/April 1982): 76-84.

[9]Peterson, Kozmetsky, and Albaum, p. 14.

[10]Irving Kristol, *Reflections of a Neoconservative* (New York: Basic Books, 1983).

[11]Richard F. Beltramini, Robert A. Peterson, and George Kozmetsky, "Public Opinion Regarding Economic Education in the Classroom," *Journal of Education for Business,* Vol. 61 (October 1985): 34-37.

3

Attitudes toward Capitalism

As noted earlier, capitalism is a cornerstone of American society; it has shaped the cultural, economic, political, and social milieu of American life. But what is the attitude of the "average American" toward this cornerstone? To understand American attitudes toward capitalism, it is necessary to query the general public, not only as a whole, but also various segments or demographic subgroups.

The major opinion polls take a broad view of public attitudes. As such, their results, while informative, too often provide only a general overview of attitudes without adequately taking into account differences and similarities among segments.

It is reasonable to assume that different segments of the population will display different attitudes toward capitalism. If this assumption is true, knowledge of such differences will be useful when developing better means of communication and understanding. A well-informed populace is necessary to develop good leadership, and since different segments may listen in different ways, information may need to be provided in a different form to each segment. Thus, the purpose of this chapter is to present the results of a study of the attitudes of the general public toward capitalism. Included is an examination of the effect of demographic characteristics on perceptions, so as to provide a *benchmark* for interpreting attitudes toward capitalism.[1] For comparison purposes, the attitudes of one influential group—business and financial editors of newspapers—were also examined. Additionally, a nationwide sample of "future leaders," college students, was also interviewed regarding their attitudes toward capitalism to provide yet another comparison basis.[2]

Newspaper business editors constitute a group that can influence public attitudes. There is virtual consensus that the news media have had, and continue to have, a major influence on public perceptions of business. The controversy arises over whether the news media have been biased in their presentation. Unfortunately, there are no objective data available. Yet, as will be shown in the next section, about 61 percent of a national general public sample perceived the news media as being *very* or *somewhat biased* in their treatment of business. An interesting additional finding, though, was that the surveyed individuals were about evenly split on the direction of bias—whether the bias was for or against business. In contrast, a survey of newspaper business editors found that about 31 percent of the sampled individuals believed the media were biased in their treatment of business. Of the 31 percent, 71 percent stated the bias was against business.

If the attitudes of this influential group toward capitalism, as a construct and a system, are essentially negative, this would explain, in part, their alleged negative attitudes toward business, the most obvious beneficiary and manifestation of capitalism. If newspaper editors whose primary subject matter is business are unfavorably disposed toward the underlying construct giving rise to their subject matter, then it would be logical for them to possess negative attitudes toward business in general, and individual firms and organizations in particular. Alternatively, if newspaper business editors are not negatively predisposed toward capitalism, *per se*, then other explanations must be sought for their alleged "antibusiness" attitudes.

The existence of bias should not be surprising, for as Califano and Simons point out:

> There can be no such thing as an objective press. This is so because there is no way an editor or a publisher can squeeze the inculcation of a lifetime from a reporter or an editor. And these inculcations—parentage, regionalism, education, friends, religion, experiences, ad infinitum—subliminally shape every story and subliminally suggest what a reporter leaves in or omits from a given story.[3]

Although strict objectivity may be lacking, and indeed, may not be possible, evidence exists that in their treatment of business, the news media attempt to be "fair." However, fairness generally is confined primarily to entertaining all sides of an issue and then making an independent judgment as to what to report rather than reporting and giving equal coverage to each side of an issue.

A BENCHMARKING PROCESS

Because of the transitional, and even transformational, nature of American society during the 1980s, a benchmark analysis of American attitudes toward capitalism is both informative and important. If American attitudes toward capitalism are changing, then we need to know in what ways in order to better understand the future problems and concerns facing the nation. Whose attitudes are changing? Are the attitudes of leaders ahead of or behind those of the general public? Are future leaders' attitudes different from those of the general public? What groups in American society can be identified as being disposed toward or against capitalism? If we can identify attitudes toward capitalism more clearly, then we can better gauge the future prospects of the system.

In benchmarking the attitudes of a society, one particular societal segment merits special attention—"future leaders," or college students. College students have long been a focus of research and speculation in evaluations of future societal directions and trends. This is so for two reasons. First, college students represent an elite element in society. As such, they are of interest in and of themselves. Frequently college students are among the first to accept, adopt, and reflect various changes or manifestations in public attitudes, values, beliefs, and norms. At times, college students serve as the vehicle for evolutionary trends in society. Collectively, they can be considered a barometer for future social changes.

Second, today's college students are tomorrow's business and government leaders. Much of what these future leaders will undertake or bring to bear on societal problems, whether in the public or private sector, has already been determined or is currently in the process of being shaped during their educational experiences. For such reasons it is instructive to measure their attitudes toward capitalism. Doing so provides potentially valuable insights, not only into their present values, but also their future behaviors.

How Attitudes Were Assessed

General Public. To assess attitudes toward capitalism, the benchmarking study targeted middle-class adults in the United States as the population of interest. Data were obtained in 1980 by mail survey techniques through the auspices of a national panel organization. Specifically, a questionnaire was mailed to a random sample of 2,400 households that were selected from this panel.[4] Responses were received from 1,556 individuals, representing a response rate of 65 percent. The study did not use preliminary notification or follow-up techniques. Data were subsequently weighted by census information pertaining to gender and age to arrive at an obtained sample that can be described as representing "middle-class adults."

Sample members provided data regarding their attitudes toward capitalism by responding to a set of sixteen Likert-type items. Each item consisted of a declarative statement followed by a six-point numerical scale that was verbally anchored by "strongly agree" and "strongly disagree."

The attitude statements were derived from several sources. Some were obtained by content-analyzing the writings of several well-known capitalism authors; others were derived from responses to a national poll that examined alternative economic systems (see Chapter 2).

Analysis of responses was carried out for all respondents as a group and for selected demographic subgroups. Aggregate results give at best a broad view of public attitudes and concerns. It seems reasonable to assume that different segments of a society can have different attitudes toward that society's basic institutions. Consequently, there is merit in examining the extent to which people's attitudes toward capitalism differ by such personal characteristics as gender, age, education, income, and marital status.

Business editors. Data were also collected in 1980 from a sample of newspaper business and financial editors by means of a mail survey. Specifically, questionnaires were mailed to the business-financial editors of 1,027 newspapers in the United States. Business-financial editors were selected for study because they are, to a certain extent, gatekeepers with respect to what (and how much) business information is reported in the nation's newspapers. Moreover, many, if not most, newspaper business and financial editors double as reporters and writers (especially those employed by smaller or medium-sized newspapers). Hence, in their two roles, gatekeeper and reporter, they directly determine the business news coverage of their newspapers.

After two follow-up mailings, 454 usable questionnaires were obtained for analysis, representing an effective response rate of 52 percent. Approximately 85 percent of the editors responding to the survey were male. More than half, 51 percent, were less than 35 years old; 25 percent were in the 35-49 age group, and 24 percent were 50 years of age or older. About 86 percent of the survey respondents were college graduates. Interestingly, less than half of the editors surveyed had received a college degree in journalism; two-thirds reported taking two or more business courses while in college. Forty-five percent of the respondents had been business editors for two or fewer years, 25 percent had been in that occupational category 3-6 years, 11 percent for 7-10 years, and 19 percent more than 10 years. Because a disproportionate number of the editors were associated with newspapers having circulations of less than 100,000, for purposes of analysis the data were weighted to reflect national newspaper circulation figures.

Future leaders. To obtain data on the attitudes of "future leaders" toward capitalism, data were collected in 1980 from a sample of 2,856 college students attending 28 different universities located in 23 different states. Both public and private institutions were included. For the most part, the universities included in the sample represented "upper tier" educational institutions and are among the most prominent universities in their respective states. Hence, while the universities cannot be thought of as representative of all colleges and universities in the United States, they provide a solid nexus of those institutions in which future generations of business, social, and political leaders are likely to be educated.

Because the study addressed a variety of issues, only five attitude statements regarding capitalism were included in the questionnaire. Although the questionnaires were self-administered, at each university a faculty member was requested to assume responsibility for obtaining a representative sample of students from three academic disciplines: business, liberal arts or social science, and engineering or natural sciences. The resulting data were weighted using Census Bureau statistics to reflect 1980 university enrollments. In the three fields of study in the analysis sample, 54 percent of the students surveyed were male; 20 percent majored in business, 52 percent majored in liberal arts or social sciences, and 28 percent majored in engineering or natural sciences. Forty-six percent of the students classified themselves as seniors, 35 percent as juniors, 12 percent as sophomores, and 7 percent as freshmen.

PRELIMINARY ANALYSIS

To place the survey respondents' attitudes toward capitalism in perspective, the general public and business editors sampled were queried about their perceptions of news media bias toward business and whether their attitude toward business had changed in recent years. Specifically, individuals in both groups were asked whether they believed the news media present an unbiased or biased view of business (and, if so, whether the bias is for or against business), and whether their attitude toward business had become more positive or more negative in recent years. Table 3.1 presents the results of asking these questions.

As might be expected, more than two-thirds of the business editors perceived the news media to be unbiased in their presentation of business. Simultaneously, though, fewer than 4 out of 10 general public respondents held this perception. Somewhat surprising was the finding that, among the editors perceiving news media bias, 71 percent perceived the bias to be against business, whereas within the general public there was about an equal split in reported perception as to whether the news media were biased for or against business. Table 3.1 also reveals that the editors' attitude toward business had generally become more positive with the passage of time. Nearly 9 out of 10 responding editors stated their attitude had become either somewhat more (75 percent) or much more (13 percent) positive in recent years. General public respondents were not nearly as positive; only 50 percent indicated their attitude toward business had become either much

Table 3.1   Perceptions of News Media Bias and Changes in Attitudes toward Business

Question	Percentage Response*	
	Business Editors	General Public
News media view of business	(n=435)	(n=1,412)
Very unbiased	5.7	4.9
Somewhat unbiased	62.8	34.5
Somewhat biased	27.1	49.4
Very biased	4.4	11.2
Direction of bias	(n=167)	(n=930)
Strongly for business	3.6	9.8
Somewhat for business	25.1	42.8
Somewhat against business	61.7	42.1
Strongly against business	9.6	5.3
Change in attitude toward business	(n=372)	(n=1,414)
Much more positive	12.6	10.8
Somewhat more positive	75.3	39.0
Somewhat more negative	11.6	42.6
Much more negative	0.5	7.6

*All respective response distributions are significantly different at p<.001 using a χ^2 test. Sample sizes within a group differ because of item omissions by individual respondents.

more or somewhat more positive in recent years. Although the reported attitude change difference between the two groups is statistically significant, it must be interpreted with some caution, since the initial attitude bases may have been substantially different (i.e., editors may have been much more negative initially).

A further preliminary insight into attitudes toward capitalism can be obtained by examining reported confidence in the American economic system. More than 80 percent of the responding editors reported having quite a lot (43 percent) or a great deal (40 percent) of confidence in the American economic system, whereas 61 percent of the general public sample held this view, a difference that is statistically significant (p<.001). Relatively fewer business editors (1 percent) than members of the general public (9 percent) stated that they had very little confidence in the American economic system.

A final comparison of the general public with business editor respondents relates to their social and political philosophies. Such philosophies can either affect or simply be a reflection of attitudes toward capitalism. As shown in Table 3.2, about 63 percent of the general public respondents stated that they were politically conservative, while nearly 41 percent were socially liberal. Combining the two philosophies shows that 29 percent of the general public respondents can be categorized as both politically and socially liberal, whereas 51 percent were politically and socially conservative.

Sixty percent of the business editors stated they were politically conservative, whereas 57 percent reported being socially liberal. About one-third of the respondent editors can be categorized as politically and socially liberal, with another one-third being politically and socially conservative. Interestingly, 8 percent of the editors reported themselves as being politically liberal and socially conservative, as compared with 9 percent of the general public.

WHAT THE PUBLIC THINKS

Table 3.3 presents the sixteen attitude items used in the investigation as well as the percentages of the general public and newspaper business editors sampled agreeing with each one.[5] From these data it is apparent that statistically significant differences ($p < .001$) exist between the two groups on eleven of the sixteen statements. Differences in agreement percentages between the groups range from less than 2 percentage points to more than 23 percentage points, with the average difference being 12 percentage points.

The greatest difference between the groups exists for the statement "capitalism must be altered before any significant improvements in human welfare can be realized." The greatest similarity in agreement occurred for two items, "efficient management can only be achieved through capitalism" and "capitalism provides maximum benefits for society as a whole."

In general, the responses of the editors indicate they were favorably disposed toward capitalism in an absolute sense. At the same time, they were also relatively more favorably disposed toward capitalism than was the general public. In fact, there was virtual consensus among the editors that

- capitalism does not deny the masses property in life, liberty, and estate;
- a free society can exist under a capitalistic system;
- a capitalistic system advocates the work ethic and the free market mechanism;

Table 3.2   Classification of General Public and Editors According to Political and Social Philosophies

Political Philosophy	Social Philosophy (Percentage Response)					
	Liberal		Conservative		Total	
	Editors	General Public	Editors	General Public	Editors	General Public
Liberal	32.3	28.5	8.1	8.6	40.4	37.1
Conservative	24.2	12.1	35.4	50.8	59.6	62.9
Total	56.5	40.6	43.5	59.4	100.0	100.0

- capitalism provides people with personal incentives to make the most productive use of their assets; and
- capitalists are entitled to the reward of profits because they assume the risk of loss.

Moreover, detailed analysis of the data reveals that the editors were more homogeneous in their attitudes toward capitalism than was the general public.

Although the general public sample was, in an absolute sense, favorably disposed toward capitalism, responses suggest at least a portion was somewhat disaffected. There was concern expressed for the system's efficiency, its effect on human welfare, and the influence of large companies. More than one-fourth believed that "capitalism denies the masses property in life, liberty, and estate." In addition, over one-third of the sample questioned whether "capitalism is the most efficient economic system the world has ever known," whether "capitalism provides maximum benefits for society as a whole," and whether "capitalism encourages the efficient use of economic resources."

Responses of the general public sample were also analyzed as to their relationship with five demographic variables: gender, age, education, income level, and marital status. After reporting the responses for each of these variables, a cross-sectional profile for each of the sixteen attitudinal statements is presented.

Table 3.3   Attitudes of General Public and Business Editors toward Capitalism

Attitude Item	Percentage Agreement	
	General Public	Business Editors
Capitalism denies the masses property in life, liberty, and estate.*	24.0	4.4
A capitalistic system advocates the work ethic and the free market mechanism.*	81.6	94.2
A free society can exist under a capitalistic system.*	77.3	95.0
Efficient management can only be achieved through capitalism.	57.4	58.4
Capitalists are entitled to the reward of profits because they assume the risk of loss.*	78.3	93.4
Capitalism is the most efficient economic system the world has ever known.*	68.0	78.3
Capitalism provides maximum benefits for society as a whole.	66.4	66.9
Capitalism is more than an economic system—it is a complex of institutions, attitudes and cultures.*	83.5	89.3
Capitalism basically relies on self-interest.*	77.5	89.6
Capitalism provides people with personal incentives to make the most productive use of their assets.*	81.3	93.9
Capitalism must be altered before any significant improvements in human welfare can be realized.*	38.4	17.6
Capitalism encourages the efficient use of economic resources.*	66.1	81.2
The growth of the large corporation as the dominant form of business organization has endangered the existence of capitalism.	54.9	58.8
Capitalism encourages individual freedom of thought, choice, and action.	76.9	86.3
In a capitalistic society, every individual has an opportunity to develop his/her own special abilities.	76.3	68.8
Capitalism provides people with the highest living standard in the world.*	77.0	83.7

*Response difference is statistically significant at p<.001 using a t-test on mean scale values.

Demographic Analysis

Table 3.4 contains the percentage agreement with each of the sixteen attitude statements for nineteen demographic subgroups.   Results for each demographic subgroup are briefly highlighted below.

Gender. Women play a direct, diverse, and increasingly important role in American society.   As more career opportunities open for women and as women become even more influential as policy and decision makers, it is important to understand how their attitudes toward capitalism are similar to, or different from, those of men.

Female respondents had agreement levels different from male respondents on each of the sixteen attitude statements. Overall, females were less favorably disposed toward capitalism than were males. For all but one of the statements investigated, differences were statistically significant. Only for the statement "the growth of the large corporation as the dominant form of business organization has endangered the existence of capitalism" is there no significant difference in agreement levels.

Although there are statistically significant differences ($p < .001$) between men and women for the statements, on an *absolute* basis both groups held positive attitudes toward capitalism. Only on a *relative* basis were females more negatively disposed toward capitalism than were males.

The consistency of attitudinal differences between the men and women studied and their significance lead to interesting speculations as to whether education or other societal or cultural characteristics cause women to be more critical of capitalism than men. However, as previously noted, this research was not designed to provide the answers to such questions. Its scope was much more limited—providing a benchmark. If more detailed insights into the relationship between gender and capitalism attitudes (e.g., the role of women, both as attitude-holders and attitude-influencers) are required, additional research needs to be conducted.

Age. Political movements, revolutions, and philosophical reforms have repeatedly been initiated and supported by younger societal members. Traditionally, older individuals are more likely to possess conservative attitudes, whereas younger individuals are more likely to possess idealistic and liberal attitudes. However, research recently has found the present generation of youth (18-25 years of age) tends to be relatively more conservative than its predecessors, signifying perhaps a "structural change" in the relationship between age and political and social conservatism/ liberalism.

Across the five age groups studied, several statistically significant differences were observed. In general, the 45-54 age group consistently displayed more favorable attitudes toward capitalism than any other age

Table 3.4   Attitudes of General Public toward Capitalism by Gender, Age, Education, Income, and Marital Status

	Percentage Agreement Gender	
Attitude Item	Male	Female
Capitalism denies the masses property in life, liberty, and estate.*	17.0	32.3
A capitalistic system advocates the work ethic and the free market mechanism.*	86.8	75.5
A free society can exist under a capitalistic system.*	84.6	69.3
Efficient management can only be achieved through capitalism. *	62.3	52.1
Capitalists are entitled to the reward of profits because they assume the risk of loss.*	85.8	69.6
Capitalism is the most efficient economic system the world has ever known.*	74.3	60.6
Capitalism provides maximum benefits for society as a whole.*	69.4	62.0
Capitalism is more than an economic system—it is a complex of institutions, attitudes, and cultures.*	87.7	79.0
Capitalism basically relies on self-interest.*	81.1	72.7
Capitalism provides people with personal incentives to make the most productive use of their assets.*	87.7	74.8
Capitalism must be altered before any significant improvements in human welfare can be realized.*	31.0	47.1
Capitalism encourages the efficient use of economic resources.*	68.7	62.4
The growth of the large corporation as the dominant form of business organization has endangered the existence of capitalism.	53.2	56.5
Capitalism encourages individual freedom of thought, choice, and action.*	83.3	70.4
In a capitalistic society, every individual has an opportunity to develop his/her own special abilities.*	82.9	70.1
Capitalism provides people with the highest living standard in the world.*	83.3	69.7

Table 3.4 (continued)

Attitude Item	Percentage Agreement Age				
	25-34	35-44	45-54	55-64	65 and over
Capitalism denies the masses property in life, liberty, and estate.*	25.0	25.2	16.9	28.4	30.4
A capitalistic system advocates the work ethic and the free market mechanism.*	80.4	81.7	86.5	80.2	76.3
A free society can exist under a capitalistic system.*	75.7	75.6	82.0	75.0	74.2
Efficient management can only be achieved through capitalism.	51.0	54.2	65.0	58.7	59.5
Capitalists are entitled to the reward of profits because they assume the risk of loss.*	78.8	76.1	80.5	73.5	75.5
Capitalism is the most efficient economic system the world has ever known.*	61.9	62.8	72.3	69.7	70.6
Capitalism provides maximum benefits for society as a whole.	61.9	64.6	73.0	65.4	68.3
Capitalism is more than an economic system—it is a complex of institutions, attitudes, and cultures.*	83.6	84.1	84.4	82.8	78.9
Capitalism basically relies on self-interest.*	78.0	78.0	76.9	78.6	71.3
Capitalism provides people with personal incentives to make the most productive use of their assets.*	79.0	82.0	83.6	80.4	78.5
Capitalism must be altered before any significant improvements in human welfare can be realized.*	38.3	42.3	33.8	40.4	44.8
Capitalism encourages the efficient use of economic resources.*	61.0	62.5	69.6	67.8	71.0
The growth of the large corporation as the dominant form of business organization has endangered the existence of capitalism.	54.1	51.5	57.6	52.1	52.1
Capitalism encourages individual freedom of thought, choice, and action.	74.9	74.6	81.6	76.9	74.4
In a capitalistic society, every individual has an opportunity to develop his/her own special abilities.	74.7	72.4	79.4	76.1	75.3
Capitalism provides people with the highest living standard in the world.*	73.0	76.3	80.4	77.0	76.0

Table 3.4 (continued)

Attitude Item	Percentage Agreement Education Level			
	Less than high school	High school	Some college	College graduate
Capitalism denies the masses property in life, liberty, and estate.*	41.8	30.9	21.9	18.3
A capitalistic system advocates the work ethic and the free market mechanism.*	62.9	75.1	85.1	86.9
A free society can exist under a capitalistic system.*	58.4	69.8	78.6	85.1
Efficient management can only be achieved through capitalism.	46.5	51.0	61.1	62.1
Capitalists are entitled to the reward of profits because they assume the risk of loss.*	54.3	70.3	78.2	85.0
Capitalism is the most efficient economic system the world has ever known.*	54.9	60.7	73.2	69.7
Capitalism provides maximum benefits for society as a whole.	57.8	62.0	69.0	67.5
Capitalism is more than an economic system—it is a complex of institutions, attitudes, and cultures.*	71.5	78.9	84.5	89.0
Capitalism basically relies on self-interest.*	71.2	71.2	78.1	81.5
Capitalism provides people with personal incentives to make the most productive use of their assets.*	68.6	75.9	82.8	86.8
Capitalism must be altered before any significant improvements in human welfare can be realized.*	49.8	46.2	39.7	32.4
Capitalism encourages the efficient use of economic resources.*	63.0	60.4	66.8	69.1
The growth of the large corporation as the dominant form of business organization has endangered the existence of capitalism.	53.2	56.0	55.8	54.0
Capitalism encourages individual freedom of thought, choice, and action.	64.5	69.3	81.0	82.2
In a capitalistic society, every individual has an opportunity to develop his/her own special abilities.	61.8	71.2	81.4	79.2
Capitalism provides people with the highest living standard in the world.*	60.3	70.1	80.1	82.6

Table 3.4 (continued)

Attitude Item	Percentage Agreement Income: Under $10,000	$10,000 - $14,999	$15,000 - $19,999	$20,000 - $24,999	$25,000 & over
Capitalism denies the masses property in life, liberty, and estate.*	37.8	28.1	24.6	18.6	17.8
A capitalistic system advocates the work ethic and the free market mechanism.*	71.5	78.3	83.0	84.2	86.1
A free society can exist under a capitalistic system.*	58.7	70.7	72.9	84.7	82.1
Efficient management can only be achieved through capitalism.	49.8	53.7	56.2	59.8	62.7
Capitalists are entitled to the reward of profits because they assume the risk of loss.*	67.0	75.9	76.8	81.6	82.0
Capitalism is the most efficient economic system the world has ever known.*	60.3	65.8	63.5	71.4	71.0
Capitalism provides maximum benefits for society as a whole.	72.7	67.4	60.9	69.6	69.9
Capitalism is more than an economic system—it is a complex of institutions, attitudes, and cultures.*	77.4	84.0	83.1	85.3	85.6
Capitalism basically relies on self-interest.*	70.0	76.3	76.7	78.6	79.9
Capitalism provides people with personal incentives to make the most productive use of their assets.*	72.7	80.7	77.3	88.6	85.1
Capitalism must be altered before any significant improvements in human welfare can be realized.*	48.6	46.7	34.8	40.8	33.3
Capitalism encourages the efficient use of economic resources.*	62.8	61.4	62.7	67.4	69.4
The growth of the large corporation as the dominant form of business organization has endangered the existence of capitalism.	55.4	53.5	58.3	59.5	52.3
Capitalism encourages individual freedom of thought, choice, and action.	69.2	76.3	71.8	76.5	83.4
In a capitalistic society, every individual has an opportunity to develop his/her own special abilities.	68.0	76.0	72.0	77.9	82.1
Capitalism provides people with the highest living standard in the world.*	66.6	75.6	74.8	81.0	81.6

Table 3.4 (continued)

Attitude Item	Percentage Agreement Marital Status		
	Married	Never married	Other
Capitalism denies the masses property in life, liberty, and estate.*	28.2	20.0	31.7
A capitalistic system advocates the work ethic and the free market mechanism.*	80.3	88.4	74.6
A free society can exist under a capitalistic system.*	74.6	84.8	73.6
Efficient management can only be achieved through capitalism.	57.8	56.4	52.2
Capitalists are entitled to the reward of profits because they assume the risk of loss.*	75.9	83.7	72.0
Capitalism is the most efficient economic system the world has ever known.*	67.4	63.9	63.8
Capitalism provides maximum benefits for society as a whole.	67.0	64.1	60.2
Capitalism is more than an economic system—it is a complex of institutions, attitudes, and cultures.*	87.2	79.1	82.8
Capitalism basically relies on self-interest.*	75.1	82.8	74.2
Capitalism provides people with personal incentives to make the most productive use of their assets.*	80.5	84.4	76.5
Capitalism must be altered before any significant improvements in human welfare can be realized.*	41.2	35.4	43.0
Capitalism encourages the efficient use of economic resources.*	65.7	67.5	61.3
The growth of the large corporation as the dominant form of business organization has endangered the existence of capitalism.	56.9	51.5	52.1
Capitalism encourages individual freedom of thought, choice, and action.	75.0	82.8	73.7
In a capitalistic society, every individual has an opportunity to develop his/her own special abilities.	75.4	77.2	73.4
Capitalism provides people with the highest living standard in the world.*	75.6	79.5	72.2

*Subgroup responses significantly different at p<.001 using an F-test.

group. The 65 and over age group was significantly less favorable toward capitalism than any other group on nine of the sixteen statements. The 25-35 age group was also generally less favorably disposed toward capitalism.

Age, therefore, is not by itself monotonically related to favorable attitudes toward capitalism. However, age appears to be an important factor in differentiating population segments as to their socioeconomic and political attitudes. It is very difficult to guess the factors that may cause discrepancies in attitudes between age groups. It is to be expected that younger (perhaps more idealistic) individuals would feel relatively less favorable toward capitalism than older individuals. A somewhat unexpected result is the finding that the oldest age group (65 and over) displayed less favorable attitudes toward capitalism than the three middle age groups. Although there does not appear to be an obvious explanation for the similarity of attitudes held by the youngest and oldest age subgroups, perhaps the oldest group is having an influence over the "youth" (or vice versa) of which it is not even aware. On the other hand, the relationship may be spurious. Similar to the gender variable, more research is required.

Education. There appears to be a direct relationship between level of education and attitudes toward capitalism. Respondents with at least a college degree reported the most favorable attitudes toward capitalism, whereas respondents with less than a high school degree appeared to be the least favorably disposed toward it.

At least one-half of the respondents in each of the education subgroups agreed that "the growth of the large corporation as the dominant form of business organization has endangered the existence of capitalism." There is not a significant difference among the four education groups on this attitude statement. The large corporation (i.e., "big business") appears to be considered primarily responsible for the perceived decay of capitalism.

Regardless of educational attainment, though, nearly half (45 percent) of the general public respondents were favorably disposed toward capitalism. Moreover, among respondents with a college degree, at least 62 percent possessed favorable attitudes toward capitalism on all sixteen statements.

Schumpeter predicted that the more educated elites would teach the masses to resent the capitalistic system as it matures.[6] He also believed that as a capitalistic system matures, business people will have less will to defend capitalism. This was, in his view, the way capitalism would disappear. The present results appear to contradict Schumpeter's forecast. If capitalism is viewed negatively in the United States, it is because of the negative attitudes mainly held by the less educated, not those more highly educated. Although the present results do not provide an explanation for the relationship between attitudes and education, it is possible to speculate that individuals with higher educational levels may have a better understanding of capitalism and therefore be more favorable toward it. Additionally, more educated segments of society may feel more comfortable with the status quo than do less educated segments, who have fewer economic opportunities available within the present social structure. As before, more research is necessary.

Household Income. It was expected intuitively that higher income respondents would be more favorable toward capitalism than those with lower incomes. Table 3.4 affirms this expectation, albeit with some notable variations. In certain instances, income and attitudes toward capitalism do not appear to be directly related.

The higher their income, the *less* respondents agreed with the statement "capitalism denies the masses property in life, liberty, and estate." Also, the higher their income, the *more* respondents agreed with the statements that capitalism advocates the work ethic, that a free society exists under a capitalistic system, that efficient management can only be achieved through capitalism, that capitalists are entitled to the reward of profits because they assume the risk of loss, and that capitalism basically relies on self-interest.

Respondents in the $10,000-$14,999 income category showed somewhat more favorable attitudes toward capitalism than those in the next higher income bracket. They were more likely to agree that capitalism is the most efficient economic system in the world, that it is more than an economic system, that it provides people with personal incentives to make the most productive use of their assets, that it encourages individual freedom of thought, choice, and action, that in a capitalistic society every individual has an opportunity to develop his or her own special abilities, and that capitalism provides people with the highest living standard in the world.

Respondents in the lowest income category responded more favorably toward the statement that capitalism provides maximum benefits for society as a whole than did respondents in the two income categories immediately above. Respondents in the $10,000-$14,999 income category appeared to be less favorable toward the idea that capitalism encourages the efficient use of economic resources than respondents in the income categories immediately above and below them. There appears to be no pattern in the way respondents with different income levels responded to the statement that capitalism must be altered before any significant improvements in human welfare can be realized.

In brief, although respondents in the two highest income categories investigated consistently displayed more favorable attitudes toward capitalism than did those in lower income categories, there seems to be less consistency with regard to the attitudes of the latter three income groups. It is important to note that differences in attitudes toward capitalism across income levels are significant for eleven of the sixteen items. Even so, the majority of respondents in all income categories report favorable attitudes toward capitalism on an absolute basis.   Hence, the general notion that differences in income will ultimately destroy capitalism does not find support in the data reported here.[7]

Marital Status. Table 3.4 also shows the attitudes toward capitalism of respondents who were married, had never been married, and other (i.e., widowed, divorced). There are few significant differences in the responses of the three groups. In general, the individuals who were married were more likely to be favorably disposed toward capitalism than were individuals in the remaining groups. Analogous to previous subgroup analyses, the results reveal that all three groups held favorable attitudes toward capitalism in an absolute sense.

Profiling the Public

The statements used in this research represent three dimensions of capitalism—economic, social, and political. To obtain more insights into capitalism attitudes, the (hypothetical) individuals who are likely to be the most and least favorably disposed toward capitalism are profiled for each of the sixteen attitude statements. These profiles are contained in Tables 3.5 through 3.7.

Looking first at the economic dimension (Table 3.5), the individual who is most favorably disposed toward capitalism can be described as a 45- to 54-year old male with at least some college education who earns at least $25,000 per year. In contrast, the individual who is least favorably disposed toward capitalism is a female 65 years of age or older with less than a high school degree who possesses a relatively low income.

Examination of the social dimension (Table 3.6) reveals that the person most favorably inclined toward capitalism is similar to the person found using the economic dimension. The least favorably inclined is a female, over 65 years of age, with less than a high school degree and relatively low income.

Finally, the individual who is most favorable toward capitalism in terms of the political dimension is a 45- to 54-year old male who is at least a college graduate earning more than $20,000 annually. The least favorably inclined individual is characterized as the same as for the social dimension (see Table 3.7).

WHAT THE EDITORS THINK

Table 3.3 presented agreement percentages for the newspaper business editors for each of the sixteen attitude statements. To obtain more insights

Table 3.5   Economic Dimension Profile

Attitude Item	Demographic Characteristic				
	Gender	Age	Education	Income	Marital status
Most favorably disposed					
A capitalistic system advocates the work ethic and the free market mechanism.	Male	45-54	College+	$25,000+	Never Married
Efficient management can exist under a capitalistic system.	Male	45-54	College+	$25,000+	Married
Capitalists are entitled to the reward of profits because they assume the risk of loss	Male	45-54	College+	$25,000+	Never Married
Capitalism is the most efficient economic system the world has ever known.	Male	45-54	Some College	$20,000-$24,999	Married
Capitalism provides people with personal incentives to make the most productive use of their assets.	Male	45-54	College+	$20,000-$24,999	Never Married
Capitalism encourages freedom of thought, choice, and action.	Male	65+	College+	$25,000+	Never Married
The growth of the large corporation as the dominant form of business organization has endangered the existence of capitalism.	Male	35-44	Less than high school	$25,000+	Never Married
Capitalism provides people with the highest living standard in the world.	Male	45-54	College+	$25,000+	Never Married

into their attitudes toward capitalism, responses to the sixteen statements were analyzed on the basis of gender, age, highest education level attained, and number of years of experience as a business editor. The results of doing so are reported in Tables 3.8 and 3.9.

Although male editors tended to possess more favorable attitudes toward capitalism than did female editors, there are only three statements

Table 3.5 (continued)

Attitude Item	Demographic Characteristic				
	Gender	Age	Education	Income	Marital status
Least favorably disposed					
A capitalistic system advocates the work ethic and the free market mechanism.	Female	65+	Less than high school	Under $10,000	Other
Efficient management can exist under a capitalistic system.	Female	25-34	Less than high school	Under $10,000	Other
Capitalists are entitled to the reward of profits because they assume the risk of loss.	Female	55-64	Less than high school	Under $10,000	Other
Capitalism is the most efficient economic system the world has ever known.	Female	25-34	Less than high school	Under $10,000	Other
Capitalism provides people with personal incentives to make the most productive use of their assets.	Female	65+	Less than high school	Under $10,000	Other
Capitalism encourages freedom of thought, choice, and action.	Female	25-34	High school	$10,000-$19,999	Other
The growth of the large corporation as the dominant form of business organization has endangered the existence of capitalism.	Male	45-54	High school	$20,000-$24,999	Married
Capitalism provides people with the highest living standard in the world.	Male	25-34	Less than high school	Under $10,000	Other

for which statistically significant differences ($p < .05$) exist between the two groups.[8] In each case, the female editors were relatively more negative toward capitalism than were the male editors. For example, less than 30 percent of the female editors, as compared with 70 percent of the male editors, agreed that capitalism provides maximum benefits to society as a whole. Similarly, twice as many female editors (32 percent) as male editors (16 percent) believed that capitalism must be altered before there can be

Table 3.6   Social Dimension Profile

Attitude Item	Demographic Characteristic				
	Gender	Age	Education	Income	Marital status
Most favorably disposed					
Capitalism denies the masses property in life, liberty, and estate.	Male	45-54	College+	$25,000+	Never Married
A capitalistic system advocates the work ethic and the free market mechanism.	Male	45-54	College+	$25,000+	Never Married
Capitalism provides maximum benefits for society as a whole.	Male	45-54	Some College	Under $10,000	Married
Capitalism is more than an economic system—it is a complex of institutions, attitudes, and cultures.	Male	45-54	College+	$25,000+	Never Married
Capitalism basically relies on self-interest.	Male	55-64	College+	$25,000+	Never Married
Capitalism must be altered before any significant improvement in human welfare can be realized.	Male	45-54	College+	$25,000+	Never Married
In a capitalistic society every individual has an opportunity to develop his/her own special abilities.	Male	45-54	Some College	$25,000+	Never Married

improvement in human welfare. Finally, relatively fewer female editors (68 percent) than male editors (82 percent) believed capitalism encourages efficient use of resources. On an absolute basis, however, both groups tended to agree with positive statements and disagree with negative statements about capitalism.

Significant attitudinal differences exist across both the age categories and education categories investigated. In general, editors over the age of

Table 3.6 (continued)

Attitude Item	Demographic Characteristic				
	Gender	Age	Education	Income	Marital status
Least favorably disposed					
Capitalism denies the masses property in life, liberty, and estate.	Female	65+	Less than high school	Under $10,000	Other
A capitalistic system advocates the work ethic and the free market mechanism.	Female	65+	Less than high school	Under $10,000	Other
Capitalism provides maximum benefits for society as a whole.	Female	25-34	Less than high school	$15,000-$19,999	Other
Capitalism is more than an economic system—it is a complex of institutions, attitudes, and cultures.	Female	65+	Less than high school	Under $10,000	Other
Capitalism basically relies on self-interest.	Female	65+	Less than high school	Under $10,000	Other
Capitalism must be altered before any significant improvement in human welfare can be realized.	Female	65+	Less than high school	Under $10,000	Other
In a capitalistic society every individual has an opportunity to develop his/her own special abilities.	Female	65+	Less than high school	Under $10,000	Other

forty-nine were more favorably disposed toward capitalism than were editors under the age of forty-nine; editors with higher levels of education were more critical of capitalism than were editors with lesser education. Despite such relative differences, however, all age and education subgroups were favorably disposed toward capitalism in an absolute sense.

The final classification variable examined as it related to attitudes toward capitalism was number of years of experience as a newspaper business editor. From Table 3.9 it is evident that significant differences in attitudes toward capitalism exist as a function of years of editorial experience. In particular, survey respondents with six or fewer years of editorial experience tended to be less favorably disposed toward capitalism

Table 3.7   Political Dimension Profile

| | Demographic Characteristic | | | | |
Attitude Item	Gender	Age	Education	Income	Marital status
Most favorably disposed					
A free society can exist under a capitalist system.	Male	45-54	College+	$20,000-$24,999	Never Married
Capitalism encourages individual freedom of thought, choice, and action.	Male	45-54	College+	$25,000+	Never Married
Least favorably disposed					
A free society can exist under a capitalist system.	Female	65+	Less than high school	Under $10,000	Other
Capitalism encourages individual freedom of thought, choice, and action.	Female	65+	Less than high school	Under $10,000	Other

than were survey respondents with seven or more years of experience. Two specific response differences illustrate this tendency:

- Thirty-four percent of the editors with two or fewer years of experience agreed that "efficient management can only be achieved through capitalism," whereas 82 percent of the editors with seven or more years of experience agreed with the statement; and
- Forty-four percent of the editors with two or fewer years of experience agreed that "capitalism provides maximum benefits for society as a whole" compared with 95 percent of the editors with 7-10 years of experience.

Although the attitude-experience relationship must be interpreted with caution because of the possibly confounding effect of age on experience, the nature (e.g., directionality) of the relationship is intriguing and suggests several interesting hypotheses.

Finally, in an attempt to understand the structure underlying the capitalism attitudes of the business editors, responses to the sixteen attitude statements were factor analyzed. The results suggest that the editors viewed capitalism in terms of the following four underlying dimensions (ordered from most dominant to least dominant):

Table 3.8 Attitudes of Editors toward Capitalism by Gender, Age, and Educational Level

| | Percentage Agreement | | | | |
| | Gender | | Age | | |
Attitude Item	Male	Female	Less than 35	35-49	More than 49
Capitalism denies the masses property in life, liberty, and estate.	3.8	10.6	9.4*	0.6	4.2
A capitalistic system advocates the work ethic and the free market mechanism.	94.0	96.3	95.8**	90.8	97.8
A free society can exist under a capitalistic system.	94.7	97.3	95.2**	92.1	99.4
Efficient management can only be achieved through capitalism.	59.2	47.7	54.5*	49.3	78.4
Capitalists are entitled to the reward of profits because they assume the risk of loss.	93.6	91.5	92.6**	90.7	98.7
Capitalism is the most efficient economic system the world has ever known.	78.2	77.0	81.4	78.7	73.8
Capitalism provides maximum benefits for society as a whole.	70.2*	29.7	61.1*	64.1	78.6
Capitalism is more than an economic system—it is a complex of institutions, attitudes, and cultures.	88.3	98.8	91.7*	81.4	99.2
Capitalism basically relies on self-interest.	88.9	95.3	95.3**	88.2	84.6
Capitalism provides people with personal incentives to make the most productive use of their assets.	93.8	95.2	93.4	91.9	97.9
Capitalism must be altered before any significant improvements in human welfare can be realized.	15.7**	32.4	29.6*	12.4	11.4
Capitalism encourages the efficient use of economic resources.	82.4**	67.6	69.5*	82.9	93.1
The growth of the large corporation as the dominant form of business organization has endangered the existence of capitalism.	60.0	45.8	67.0**	53.0	58.1
Capitalism encourages individual freedom of thought, choice, and action.	86.7	80.9	85.8*	81.0	95.7
In a capitalistic society, every individual has an opportunity to develop his/her own special abilities.	70.1	53.9	67.1*	62.0	82.2
Capitalism provides people with the highest living standard in the world.	84.3	76.0	87.2	79.0	86.9

Table 3.8 (continued)

Attitude Item	Percentage Agreement Education Level			
	Not a college graduate	College graduate	Graduate level work	Master's degree and above
Capitalism denies the masses property in life, liberty, and estate.	98.7	96.4	95.5	90.0
A capitalistic system advocates the work ethic and the free market mechanism.	98.1	98.6	95.5	90.6
A free society can exist under a capitalistic system.*	69.0	56.6	68.2	49.7
Efficient management can only be achieved through capitalism.	97.8	96.0	93.0	89.9
Capitalists are entitled to the reward of profits because they assume the risk of loss.*	97.0	69.4	87.0	73.5
Capitalism is the most efficient economic system the world has ever known.	97.0	69.4	87.0	73.5
Capitalism provides maximum benefits for society as a whole.	66.4	72.1	71.3	59.7
Capitalism is more than an economic system—it is a complex of institutions, attitudes, and cultures.	97.5	86.4	92.5	86.9
Capitalism basically relies on self-interest.	94.4	84.8	92.2	90.1
Capitalism provides people with personal incentives to make the most productive use of their assets.	95.2	97.2	94.8	90.2
Capitalism must be altered before any significant improvements in human welfare can be realized.*	3.8	28.2	18.9	12.9
Capitalism encourages the efficient use of economic resources.	88.3	80.1	83.0	78.3
The growth of the large corporation as the dominant form of business organization has endangered the existence of capitalism.*	52.3	60.0	43.6	69.7
Capitalism encourages individual freedom of thought, choice, and action.*	92.1	89.7	93.1	76.7
In a capitalistic society, every individual has an opportunity to develop his/her own special abilities.*	73.4	64.0	86.1	59.5
Capitalism provides people with the highest living standard in the world.*	97.4	80.3	92.1	76.2

*Subgroup response distributions significantly different at p<.01 using a χ^2 test.

**Subgroup response distributions significantly different at p<.05 using a χ^2 test.

Table 3.9 Attitudes of Editors toward Capitalism by Number of Years of Experience

Attitude Item	Percentage Agreement Number of years of experience			
	2 or less	3-6	7-10	More than 10
Capitalism denies the masses property in life, liberty, and estate.	8.6	2.1	4.8	0.8
A capitalistic system advocates the work ethic and the free market mechanism.	93.6	90.4	98.6	98.5
A free society can exist under a capitalistic system.**	94.3	91.1	99.8	99.2
Efficient management can only be achieved through capitalism.*	33.8	58.9	82.0	81.7
Capitalists are entitled to the reward of profits because they assume the risk of loss.	93.4	89.4	95.5	98.7
Capitalism is the most efficient economic system the world has ever known.*	74.8	65.7	91.4	96.0
Capitalism provides maximum benefits for society as a whole.*	44.4	67.7	95.2	80.5
Capitalism is more than an economic system—it is a complex of institutions, attitudes, and cultures.*	81.2	87.1	100.0	98.0
Capitalism basically relies on self-interest.*	92.8	81.2	93.3	95.8
Capitalism provides people with personal incentives to make the most productive use of their assets.*	94.3	88.5	99.2	98.5
Capitalism must be altered before any significant improvements in human welfare can be realized.*	26.9	12.9	22.9	5.6
Capitalism encourages the efficient use of economic resources.*	74.2	76.4	90.7	94.1
The growth of the large corporation as the dominant form of business organization has endangered the existence of capitalism.	57.1	67.5	56.6	47.9
Capitalism encourages individual freedom of thought, choice, and action.*	79.7	82.6	94.6	98.2
In a capitalistic society, every individual has an opportunity to develop his/her own special abilities.*	53.8	57.1	96.6	92.3
Capitalism provides people with the highest living standard in the world.**	78.7	75.4	97.2	96.1

*Subgroup response distributions significantly different at p<.01 using a χ^2 test.

**Subgroup response distributions significantly different at p<.05 using a χ^2 test.

Dimension	Statements Comprising Dimension
Efficiency, Productivity, and Individual Freedom	4, 6, 7, 12, 14, 15, 16
Freedom of Choice	2, 3, 5, 8, 9, 10
Human Welfare	1, 11
Corporate Affect	13

In contrast, factor analysis of the general public responses to the sixteen attitude statements revealed only a single, general dimension that incorporates all four dimensions found for the business editors. Hence, not only did the editors view capitalism more favorably than did the general public, they also had a more complex and discriminating perception of it (at least in terms of the dimensions investigated in this study).

The Media and Business

Significant similarities exist between the news media and business. Both have an offering (service or product) to sell. Both exert tremendous influence on society and face increasing pressure to use that influence in a socially responsible manner. And both are necessary in a democratic society. The media provide information whereas business provides for the separation of economic and political control.

Despite these similarities, there also are significant differences. These differences have tended to add "fuel" to what has been termed a growing adversarial relationship.[9] For one thing, in the eyes of editors and reporters, the predictability and stability that businesses strive for often make for dull news. Consequently, reporters are sometimes accused of seeking out or emphasizing controversy, because in controversy lies a certain amount of excitement and drama—the things that sell news. A second point of difference concerns the extent of information disclosure each desires. Businesses traditionally have preferred privacy, believing that openness and accessibility only aid competition and perhaps facilitate opportunities for government intervention. The media, on the other hand, are interested in obtaining all the facts, although often only partial reporting is done.

Given the alleged antagonistic relationship that exists between the news media and business, we asked the business and financial editors what they thought about selected aspects of media and business. This part of the study extended the work of Evans, who studied the perceptions of reporters, chief executive officers, and public affairs directors of major companies regarding the role of the press in society and the adequacy of business news coverage.[10] If the allegation that the news media are antibusiness is true, it should hold that newspaper business editors would have antibusiness attitudes. However, the data presented above suggest that business editors may not have negative attitudes toward business.

The Issues

In general, business complaints about the news media can be categorized as resulting from (1) the economic illiteracy and ignorance of reporters about business, (2) inadequate coverage of business, and (3) a lack of objectivity and fairness as well as a penchant for negativism.[11] It is not surprising that media advocates either discount the validity of such complaints or argue the emphasis given them is disproportional to their importance. They respond that inaccuracies and incompleteness in reporting are oftentimes due to the inaccessibility of business executives. Even when executives are accessible, there still remains their inherent desire for secrecy. In addition, it is claimed that business people do not understand the role of the news media in an open society.[12]

There is no question that the economic and business knowledge of journalists writing about business is a problem, especially for smaller newspapers that cannot justify (or afford) a full-time staff of business reporters. Conditions are improving, however, in that overall business coverage is getting better and more newspapers have expanded their staffs and hired more knowledgeable people to carry out business news reporting.[13]

Inadequate coverage of business revolves around issues of completeness and selective reporting. To a large extent this issue and that of antibusiness bias are related. For example, it appears to many business-people that the press seems to concentrate on negative aspects of business. The press responds to this criticism in ways similar to the following:

> Editors publish stories designed to appeal to readers, not to sell
> products, and they do so when there is a legitimate news peg,
> not necessarily when salesmen are calling on their customers.[14]

Probably the most important issue is that of bias against business, or perceived bias, and what that entails in terms of an antagonistic relationship. To begin with, it must be recognized that press attacks against business are hardly a recent phenomenon. Since the early 1900s there have been such attacks. However, the 1960s saw a new trend when specific industries, companies, products, and business practices came under attack both by social critics and the news media.[15]   Indeed, there is hardly an industry or a product that has not been criticized by the news media.[16]

One reason for the antagonism can be traced to characteristics shared by the two institutions—*social power* and *influence*. Lichter and Rothman found that each institution thinks the other has more societal influence than it does, but at the same time each wants to have more influence than the other.[17] One interpretation of these perceptions is that the media and business view themselves as competing adversaries for power and influence in American society.

The Responses

A necessary starting point for assessing whether there indeed is anti-business bias in reporting is to determine whether there are any negative attitudes toward business. This can be done by analyzing the responses provided by the business editors to eight 6-category, Likert-type statements pertaining to attitudes toward media and business issues. When interpreting the editors' attitudes about these issues, it is important to remember that results presented earlier in this chapter (e.g., Table 3.1) indicated that the majority of the editors perceived themselves to be unbiased. Where bias is perceived to exist, it is perceived to be predominantly antibusiness.

Table 3.10 shows there is relative consistency among the editors surveyed regarding their attitudes toward business. At one extreme, a minimum of two-thirds of the editors *agreed* that the news media have an obligation to criticize business, that business journalists often do not understand the complexities of business, and that the negative features of business must be explored by the news media. In contrast, 41 percent of the editors stated that the news media do a good job of explaining business activities to the public, and about 68 percent believed the media should report both good and bad news about business. Nine out of ten responding editors stated that negative features of business must be explored by the media. These findings, together with those for the first attitude statement in the table, seem to imply business editors believed the news media perform a "watchdog" and "social critic" role with regard to business. At the same time, the editors believed they were not doing a particularly good job as indicated by their responses to the second and fifth statements.

Demographic Characteristics. To obtain more insights into the editors' attitudes toward the media and business, responses to the eight statements were analyzed by gender, age, and number of years of experience as a business editor. Male and female editors differ significantly ($p<.05$) on only two statements. Relatively more female editors than male editors agreed that business is essentially antagonistic toward the media. Consistent with this finding is that slightly less than 21 percent of the female editors

Table 3.10   Editors' Attitudes toward Business

Attitude Item	Total Sample	Gender Male	Gender Female	Age Under 35	Age 35-49	Age 50 and Above
The media have an obligation to criticize business.	68.8	67.5	78.0	71.6*	75.0	56.8
Journalists who report on business activities often do not understand the complexities of their subject matter.	68.5	69.5	63.6	78.6*	68.4	54.4
In general business cooperates with the media's attempts to explain business activities to the public.	62.3	66.7*	20.5	43.1*	67.4	77.2
The media have a responsibility to protect the U.S. economic system.	38.3	39.9	20.5	29.9*	32.8	60.7
The media do a good job of explaining business profit-making activities to the public.	41.4	43.3	22.7	19.3*	53.8	49.1
Business is essentially antagonistic toward the media.	59.4	57.4*	72.3	63.4*	45.9	75.0
The media consider both good and bad news about business to be equally newsworthy.	67.7	68.0	63.6	62.1	71.7	68.2
The negative features of business must be explored by the media so that they will be seen by the public.	91.5	91.3	95.0	91.4	91.8	91.9

believed business cooperates with the news media, whereas 67 percent of the male editors believed this to be true.[18]

Statistically significant differences (p<.05) emerged for two attitude items across the age subgroups investigated. Items relating to business cooperation with the media and whether the media have a responsibility to

Table 3.10 (continued)

Attitude Item	Percentage Agreement Number of years of experience			
	2 or less	3-6	7-10	More than 10
The media have an obligation to criticize business.*	69.2	65.5	60.3	83.8
Journalists who report on business activities often do not understand the complexities of their subject matter.*	80.1	53.8	64.7	77.8
In general business cooperates with the media's attempts to explain business activities to the public.*	56.8	51.7	75.0	70.9
The media have a responsibility to protect the U.S. economic system.*	22.1	42.1	44.1	54.3
The media do a good job of explaining business profit-making activities to the public.*	44.2	38.6	55.9	28.4
Business is essentially antagonistic toward the media.*	41.1	58.6	88.2	67.9
The media consider both good and bad news about business to be equally newsworthy.	67.3	73.8	53.8	68.4
The negative features of business must be explored by the media so that they will be seen by the public.*	86.6	96.5	85.3	93.8

*Response distributions significantly different at p<.01 using a χ^2 test.

protect the economic system elicited greater agreement from editors over the age of 49 than for other age groupings. The most dramatic age differences exist for beliefs about the role of the news media in protecting the economic system. Approximately 61 percent of the editors over the age of 49 believed the news media have such responsibility, but less than 30 percent of the editors under the age of 35 and less than one-third of the editors aged 35-49 believed in this responsibility.

There are four statements for which a significant difference (p<.05) exists as a function of years of experience as a business editor. A greater percentage of editors with seven or more years of experience compared with those possessing less than seven years of experience agreed that business cooperates with the news media and the news media have a responsibility to protect the economic system. These results, of course, are consistent with those for age of editor. Although there are significant differences for the first and last attitude statements, these appear to be due to the group of responding editors with 7-10 years of experience. Compared with other respondents, a relatively smaller percentage of the group having 7-10 years of experience agreed with these two statements. The relationship between number of years of experience and response to the statement about the explanatory job done by the news media is generally the same as that found for age of editor. That is, the smallest percentage agreeing that a good job is being done was reported by editors with two or fewer years of experience.

Analyses also were conducted by educational level and, for college graduates, undergraduate major. Educational level is significantly related only to the statement "the media have a responsibility to protect the U. S. economic system." Two-thirds of the editors not graduating from college agreed with this statement, whereas only 40 percent of the editors possessing an undergraduate degree or more agreed. For college graduates, responses to the attitude statements did not differ significantly between editors majoring in journalism and those majoring in other disciplines.

Political and Social Philosophies.[19] A business editor's attitudes toward the media and business could be influenced by his/her political and/or social philosophy. Accordingly, responses to the eight attitude statements were related to the political and social philosophy variables previously discussed. The results are shown in Table 3.11.

Political philosophy significantly influences responses to six of the eight attitude statements. A greater proportion of editors who were politically liberal than those who were politically conservative agreed with the statement that the news media should criticize business and explore its negative features even though journalists do not understand the complexities of business. In contrast, a greater proportion of political conservatives than liberals agreed that business cooperates with the media even though it is antagonistic toward the media. More dramatically, almost twice as many politically conservative editors (49 percent) as liberal editors (26 percent) believed the media should protect the economic system.

Social philosophy does not have the impact on attitudes that political philosophy does; it only influences responses to two statements. In a manner similar to political philosophy, nearly twice as many socially conservative (52 percent) as liberal editors (30 percent) agreed the media have a responsibility to protect the economic system. In addition, a slightly

Table 3.11   Attitudes of Editors toward Capitalism by Political and Social Philosophy

| | Percentage Agreement | | | |
| | Political Philosophy | | Social Philosophy | |
Attitude Item	Liberal	Conservative	Liberal	Conservative
The media have an obligation to criticize business.	77.3*	61.3	68.4	67.1
Journalists who report on business activities often do not understand the complexities of their subject matter.	73.1	63.4	64.5	71.1
In general business cooperates with the media's attempts to explain business activities to the public.	57.9	68.1	63.2	64.7
The media have a responsibility to protect the U.S. economic system.	26.4*	48.5	29.6	52.3
The media do a good job of explaining business profit-making activities to the public.	38.0	45.4	41.7	43.3
Business is essentially antagonistic toward the media.	52.5*	66.1	59.8	61.9
The media consider both good and bad news about business to be equally newsworthy.	62.5	69.8	61.6	73.6
The negative features of business must be explored by the media so that they will be seen by the public.	97.3*	87.1	90.2	92.6

*Response difference is statistically significant at p<.01 using a χ^2 test.

larger percentage of conservatives (74 percent) than liberals (62 percent) agreed that the media consider both good and bad news about business to be equally newsworthy.

WHAT COLLEGE STUDENTS THINK

Table 3.12 presents the five attitude statements used in the college student investigation as well as the percentage of the college student sample

Table 3.12   Comparison of Attitudes toward Capitalism of General Public and College Students

	Percentage Agreement	
Attitude Item*	General Public	College Students
Capitalism denies the masses property in life, liberty, and estate.	24.0	36.3
A capitalistic system advocates the work ethic and the free market mechanism.	81.6	71.9
A free society can exist under a capitalistic system.	77.3	70.8
Efficient management can only be achieved through capitalism.	57.4	47.9
Capitalists are entitled to the reward of profits because they assume the risk of loss.	78.3	65.6

*Intersample responses all significantly different at p<.001 using a t-test on mean scale values.

agreeing with each one. For comparison purposes, general public agreement percentages are also included in the table. For each of the five statements, the difference in response between the two groups is statistically significant (p < .001); however, this is because of the large sample sizes as well as the underlying differences in attitudes.

In general, the college students' attitudes toward capitalism were more negative than were those of the general public. The smallest difference, 5 percentage points, occurs for "a free society can exist under a capitalistic system." The largest difference, 11 percentage points, occurs for "capitalists are entitled to the reward of profits because they assume the risk of loss."

Table 3.13 presents agreement percentages for three college student characteristics: gender, major, and academic classification. As can be seen from the table:

- Males were more positively disposed toward capitalism than were females.
- Business majors were more positively disposed toward capitalism than were liberal arts or engineering majors.
- Freshmen appeared to be slightly less favorably disposed toward capitalism than were sophomores, juniors, or seniors.

Table 3.13   Attitudes of College Students toward Capitalism by Gender, Major, and Academic Classification

| Attitude Item* | Percentage Agreement | | | | |
| | Gender | | Major | | |
	Males	Females	Busi- ness	Liberal Arts	Engin- eering
Capitalism denies the masses property in life, liberty, and estate.	32.1	35.8	30.0	37.5	37.8
A capitalistic system advocates the work ethic and the free market mechanism.	76.1	71.2	76.7	69.5	73.0
A free society can exist under a capitalistic system.	78.5*	65.6	74.9	68.1	73.7
Efficient management can only be achieved through capitalism.	52.3	45.4	51.2	45.3	50.2
Capitalists are entitled to the reward of profits because they assume the risk of loss.	74.6*	63.0	75.4*	62.7	64.1

These results are intuitively logical and, in general, corroborate the relationships previously found between capitalism attitudes and education and capitalism attitudes and gender.

CONCLUSION

This investigation of the attitudes held by middle-class Americans toward capitalism shows that while the majority of the surveyed individuals reported favorable attitudes toward capitalism, there were significant attitudinal differences across demographic segments. In particular, attitudes tended to differ as a function of age, education, and gender. The latter was consistently found to moderate capitalism attitudes; in all three studies females were more negatively disposed toward capitalism than were males.

The demise of capitalism has been predicted and announced by sociologists, philosophers and critics for many years. Heilbroner, for

Table 3.13 (continued)

| Attitude Item | Percentage Agreement | | | |
| | Academic Classification | | | |
	Freshman	Sophomore	Junior	Senior
Capitalism denies the masses property in life, liberty, and estate.	38.8	38.0	34.0	32.1
A capitalistic system advocates the work ethic and the free market mechanism.	69.1	72.0	74.0	75.1
A free society can exist under a capitalistic system.	62.5*	74.9	71.8	74.5
Efficient management can only be achieved through capitalism.	41.8*	51.4	48.3	51.0
Capitalists are entitled to the reward of profits because they assume the risk of loss.	59.5*	67.4	68.5	71.8

*Response distributions significantly different at $p<.001$ using a χ^2 test.

example, predicted that traditional capitalism would be substituted by planned capitalism.[20] Schumpeter attributed the disappearance of capitalism to the continuing expansion in systems of higher education and, hence, in the ranks of intellectuals (such as journalists and editors).[21]   Although the benchmarking research found that college students were more negatively disposed toward capitalism than was the general public, within the general public, the more education an individual possessed, the more he or she was positively disposed toward capitalism. Thus Schumpeter's hypothesis cannot be unequivocally accepted.

The defenders of capitalism attribute its survival to three major reasons: the fact that the economic system works, the increase in the standard of living, and the persistence of some of the ethical values that contributed to the formation of capitalism. In spite of these reasons, some writers still believe that the public is not as amenable toward capitalism as it was in the past.

Most forecasts of the demise of capitalism ignore demographic factors. The research reported here shows that such variables are an important indicator of trends and that they are possibly better predictors of attitudinal changes than are some of the economic factors that have been analyzed by the critics of capitalism.

At the beginning of the 1980s, capitalism was acceptable and welcome in American society. Some of its rules may have to be changed to reflect changing social conditions or the demographic composition of the general public. This part of the research indicates where questions regarding the present status of capitalism should be addressed.

Given the antibusiness sentiment attributed to the news media, the results of the research are somewhat surprising. The newspaper business editors surveyed were not only positively disposed toward capitalism in an absolute sense, but also as a group they were considerably more favorably disposed toward capitalism than was the general public. This finding, in conjunction with the findings that the editors reported their attitude toward business had become more positive in recent years and their overwhelming belief that capitalism is compatible with freedom of the press, suggests that either the alleged antibusiness sentiments of the news media do not emanate from this particular news media group or that their attitudes toward capitalism are not indicative of, or isomorphic with, their attitudes toward business. In either case, the generalized view that the news media are biased against business (and capitalism) is probably too simplistic and requires further research and refinement.

However, although the editors were more homogeneous in their attitudes toward capitalism than was the general public, unanimity was not present. Male editors tended to be more favorably disposed toward capitalism than were female editors. Likewise, older editors were more favorably disposed toward capitalism than were younger editors, and the more education an editor possessed, the less favorable was his or her attitude toward capitalism. Finally, an intriguing finding is that the more experience a survey participant possessed as an editor, the more positive were that individual's attitudes toward capitalism. This may be due to a variety of reasons. For example, attitudes may become more positive as familiarity with, and knowledge of, capitalism grows. Editors not favorably disposed toward capitalism may serve in that occupational capacity for only a relatively short period of time. Or, the relationship may be confounded because of age. Collectively, editor characteristics relating to attitudes toward capitalism suggest that, if present trends continue (e.g., more female, younger, and more educated editors), the attitudes of newspaper editors as a group may become somewhat less favorable toward capitalism. If that should occur, the business-media controversy can only intensify.

Although the results reported in this chapter are somewhat equivocal, it does appear that the editors studied believe their role is one of public observer and critic. This finding is consistent with that of Evans, who observed that reporters tend to view themselves as keepers of the public trust and regard exposing violations of it as an important component of their job.[22]

The adversarial nature of the news media and business will no doubt continue. One should not expect an end to the disagreements. The economic system requires that the news media play the role of critic while business retains its right of privacy and ability to use its best judgment to earn a profit.[23] Yet, there is need for a fresh perspective. Each "side" should try to have a more open mind and greater trust in the other. The long-run viability of each may very well reside in cooperation, particularly when confronted by third-party critics (e.g., government, social critics, etc.). Indeed, the very existence of capitalism demands such cooperation.

NOTES

[1]A benchmark is a point of reference against which phenomena such as measurements, stimuli, or judgments can be compared. It reflects a certain combination of time, place, group, and topic such that comparisons can be made with other times, places, groups, and topics. Benchmarking is an analytical tool that facilitates interpretation and generalizations of observed phenomena as well as the identification of differences among or between the phenomena.

[2]Much of the material in this chapter is based on Robert A. Peterson, George Kozmetsky, and Isabella C. M. Cunningham, "Perceptions of Media Bias Toward Business," *Journalism Quarterly,* Vol. 59 (Autumn 1982): 461-464, and Robert A. Peterson, Gerald Albaum, George Kozmetsky and Isabella C. M. Cunningham, "Attitudes of Newspaper Business Editors and General Public toward Capitalism," *Journalism Quarterly,* Vol. 61 (Spring 1984): 56-65.

[3]Joseph A. Califano, Jr. and Howard Simons, "The Businessman and the Journalist," in *The Media and Business,* ed. Howard Simons and Joseph A. Califano, Jr. (New York: Random House, 1979), pp. xvi.

[4]The sample was approximately 1 percent of the panel; the panel was constructed to possess demographic characteristics identical to the U. S. adult population.

[5]Although items were scaled using six categories ranging from "strongly agree" to "strongly disagree," only agreement percentages are presented in the tables for expository ease. Analyses, however, were conducted using all available data (i.e., chi-square analysis on response distributions, t- and F-tests on mean differences, etc.).

[6]Joseph A. Schumpeter, *Capitalism, Socialism and Democracy* (New York: Harper & Brothers, 1942).

[7]Michael Harrington, *The Twilight of Capitalism* (New York: Simon and Schuster, 1976), p. 320.

[8]Because of the relatively small size of the editor subgroups, statistical

significance criteria of .01 and .05 were deemed more appropriate than the more restrictive .001 used elsewhere.

9R. I. Divelbiss and Maurice R. Cullen, "Business, the Media, and the American Public," *MSU Business Topics*, Vol. 29 (Spring 1981): 21-28.

10Fred J. Evans, "Business and the Press: Conflicts over Roles, Fairness," *Public Relations Review*, Vol. 10 (Winter 1984): 33-42. One conclusion from this study was that business reporters tend to be more favorably disposed toward business than are general assignment reporters.

11S. Prakash Sethi, "Business and the News Media: The Paradox of Informed Understanding," *California Management Review*, Vol. 19 (Spring 1977): 52-62.

12Michael C. Jensen, "Business and the Press," in *Corporations and Their Critics*, ed. Thornton Bradshaw and David Vogel (New York: McGraw-Hill, 1981), p. 51.

13Ernest C. Hynds, "Business Coverage is Getting Better," *Journalism Quarterly*, Vol. 57 (Summer 1980): 297-304ff.

14David Finn, "Why Business has Trouble with the Media and Vice Versa," *Across the Board*, Vol. 15 (February 1978): 55.

15James P. Gannon, "Business and the Media: Breaking Down the Barriers," *Vital Speeches of the Day*, Vol. 46 (December 15, 1979): 133-136.

16A prime example is illustrated by a recent cover of *Business Week* (September 18, 1989).

17S. Robert Lichter and Stanley Rothman, "Media and Business Elites," *Public Opinion*, Vol. 4 (November/December 1981): 42-46ff.

18A cautionary note is in order when interpreting the effect of editor gender. Compared with that of male editors, the sample size of female editors was relatively small. Consequently, interpretations may be affected by sample sizes and sample size differences.

19This discussion will examine only the main effects of political and social philosophy. The sample size is too small to meaningfully investigate interactions of political and social philosophy and attitude.

20Robert L. Heilbroner, *Business Civilization in Decline* (New York: W. W. Harmen and Company, 1976), p. 38.

21Schumpeter, *Capitalism, Socialism, and Democracy*.

22Evans, pp. 33-42.

23Walter E. Hoadley, "Corporations and the Media Must Develop a Better Understanding," *Dun's Business Month*, Vol. 120 (September 1982): 45.

4

Perceptions of
Capitalism and Business

In Chapter 3, research that investigated attitudes toward capitalism was presented and discussed. This chapter extends that line of research by exploring in detail public perceptions of capitalism. The chapter consists of two distinct sections. In the first, thirteen attributes are used to characterize capitalism. To facilitate the interpretation of capitalism in the context of these attributes, they are also applied to the three constructs previously studied that are frequently viewed as synonymous with capitalism: free enterprise, private enterprise, and American enterprise. Additionally, to place the public's image of capitalism in a broader perspective, capitalism is compared with socialism and communism on the same thirteen attributes.

The second section of the chapter examines the linkage between the public's perception of capitalism and its view of business in general. Specifically, the section presents the results of studies regarding whether the public associates capitalism more with "big business" or "small business," and whether big business is perceived more or less positively than is small business.

THE IMAGE OF CAPITALISM

Chapter 2 revealed that the public appears to have a better grasp of the definitions of constructs related to capitalism than it does of capitalism itself. Although there has been much rhetoric about the matter, little empirical research has been conducted to systematically measure the American public's image of capitalism, related constructs, or even alternative constructs.

Public confidence in all major institutions, including business, has been declining in recent years, although the decline has not affected all equally.[1] The loss of confidence in business should be interpreted in the context of the major companies and the individuals who manage these companies. Concentration of power in the hands of the self-interested is viewed as inherently dangerous and untrustworthy and, rightly or wrongly, has led to resentment of *big* business. Lipset and Schneider believe that while confidence in the individuals who manage business institutions may be declining, the public does not appear to be ready yet to abandon capitalism.[2] This appears to be as true at the beginning of the 1990s as it was at the end of the 1970s.

Just what is the public's perception of capitalism? The preceding chapter revealed that overall the public is favorably disposed toward capitalism. However, the chapter did not address the manner in which the public characterizes capitalism. This chapter documents the public's image of capitalism.

The data. Data relating to the image of capitalism were collected in the national benchmark survey described in Chapter 3. An assessment of the public's image of capitalism was obtained by measuring how it characterized capitalism in terms of thirteen attributes. The attributes were derived from a content analysis of terms often used in the literature to describe and characterize capitalism. Since perceptions have meaning only in a relative sense, data were also collected for five other constructs to provide a basis for interpretation. To do this, a split-ballot approach was used such that each participant in the benchmark survey was asked to evaluate one of six constructs using the semantic differential scales contained in Table 4.1. Constructs were randomly assigned to survey participants. The constructs, together with the number of survey participants evaluating each, are presented below.

Construct	*Number of survey participants evaluating construct*
Capitalism	239
Free enterprise system	242
Private enterprise system	238
American enterprise system	247
Socialism	230
Communism	246

Because the sample sizes were limited, results are reported using mean values rather than percentage responses for each scale category and, with the exception of capitalism, not provided for demographic subgroups.

Table 4.1 Semantic Differential Scales Used in Image Measurement

is inherently inflationary	1 2 3 4 5 6 7	is not inherently inflationary
is dynamic	1 2 3 4 5 6 7	is static
is efficient in allocating resources	1 2 3 4 5 6 7	is inefficient in allocating resources
allows political freedom	1 2 3 4 5 6 7	does not allow political freedom
produces high quality products	1 2 3 4 5 6 7	produces low quality products
offers consumers good value for their money	1 2 3 4 5 6 7	offers consumers poor value for their money
is growing in prominence	1 2 3 4 5 6 7	is decreasing in prominence
promotes personal satisfaction	1 2 3 4 5 6 7	does not promote personal satisfaction
is socially equitable	1 2 3 4 5 6 7	is not socially equitable
promotes technology	1 2 3 4 5 6 7	does not promote technology
leads to high living standard	1 2 3 4 5 6 7	leads to low living standard
encourages freedom of choice	1 2 3 4 5 6 7	does not encourage freedom of choice
advocates the work ethic	1 2 3 4 5 6 7	does not advocate work ethic

CAPITALISM PERCEPTIONS

The mean values for capitalism on the attributes studied are contained in Table 4.2. On the basis of these scales, the public generally viewed capitalism as relatively dynamic, allowing political freedom, promoting personal satisfaction and technology, leading to a high living standard, encouraging freedom of choice, and advocating the work ethic.

Table 4.2 also contains index values for each attribute for several demographic subgroups: gender, age, education, and income. These index values show the relationship between the perceptions of the demographic subgroups relative to the total sample. Because the index value for the total sample is 100, values greater than 100 indicate the subgroup agrees *more* with the phrase shown than does the total sample. Index values less than 100

Table 4.2 General Public Perceptions of Capitalism

Attribute*	Total Sample Mean	Index Value Gender Male	Female
Is inherently inflationary	4.04	102	98
Is dynamic**	2.63	124	87
Is efficient in allocating resources	3.43	96	95
Allows political freedom	2.79	112	90
Produces high quality products	3.04	107	96
Offers consumers good value for their money	3.17	112	94
Is growing in world prominence	3.73	99	101
Promotes personal satisfaction**	2.79	115	91
Is socially equitable	3.44	106	95
Promotes technology**	2.19	136	84
Leads to high living standard**	2.52	117	91
Encourages freedom of choice**	2.51	129	86
Advocates the work ethic	2.57	113	91

Attribute	Index Value Age 24 or less	25-34	35-44	45-54	55-64	Over 65+
Is inherently inflationary	85	98	109	102	95	99
Is dynamic	76	90	110	109	91	109
Is efficient in allocating resources**	82	99	85	101	96	125
Allows political freedom**	86	89	93	107	92	125
Produces high quality products**	153	92	95	98	96	131
Offers consumers good value for their money**	112	95	97	95	93	123
Is growing in world prominence	77	97	97	103	91	123
Promotes personal satisfaction	90	97	100	101	95	109
Is socially equitable	108	97	91	96	98	117
Promotes technology	110	99	105	92	85	114
Leads to high living standard**	97	89	90	107	95	135
Encourages freedom of choice	86	93	99	103	86	126
Advocates the work ethic**	86	93	106	98	85	122

Table 4.2 (continued)

Attribute	Index Value			
	Less than high school	High school	Some college	College graduate
Is inherently inflationary	107	104	103	92
Is dynamic	78	100	100	107
Is efficient in allocating resources	109	94	97	99
Allows political freedom	91	90	104	109
Produces high quality products	101	93	102	107
Offers consumers good value for their money	91	94	99	110
Is growing in world prominence	113	94	101	102
Promotes personal satisfaction	96	95	102	103
Is socially equitable	106	100	90	103
Promotes technology	77	90	103	116
Leads to high living standard	92	93	99	110
Encourages freedom of choice	85	92	97	113
Advocates the work ethic	81	88	105	114

signify *less* agreement. The table reveals there are statistically significant differences ($p < .05$) between men and women for five attributes—dynamic, personal satisfaction, technology, living standard, and freedom of choice.[3] Relative to females, males especially tended to perceive capitalism as being dynamic (index values: 124 and 87), as promoting technology (index values: 136 and 86), and as encouraging freedom of choice (index values: 129 and 86). For each of these five attributes (as well as for those attributes where differences are not statistically significant), women viewed capitalism less favorably than did men. This finding is consistent with that reported in Chapter 3 on attitudes toward capitalism.

There are statistically significant differences among the age groups for six attributes. For four of these attributes—allocation of resources, political freedom, high living standard, and advocating the work ethic—the oldest age group (65 and over) tended to be the most positive and the youngest group (24 or less or 34 or less, respectively) the least positive. That is, younger individuals appeared to have a more critical view of capitalism than did older individuals. The image held by the oldest age group does not seem to be consistent with its attitudes toward capitalism (see Chapter 3), although

Table 4.2 (continued)

Attribute	Index Value					
	Household Income					
	Under $6,000	$6,000- $9,999	$10,000- $14,999	$15,000- $19,999	$20,000- $29,999	$30,000 or more
Is inherently inflationary	105	114	100	99	95	89
Is dynamic	91	83	97	91	111	122
Is efficient in allocating resources	111	100	94	95	91	108
Allows political freedom	97	83	102	103	105	103
Produces high quality products	106	95	94	94	13	102
Offers consumers good value for their money	92	90	103	99	111	104
Is growing in world prominence	108	102	105	96	96	99
Promotes personal satisfaction	84	96	102	91	112	104
Is socially equitable	86	98	109	92	106	99
Promotes technology	80	91	109	90	115	101
Leads to high living standard	103	92	95	92	111	106
Encourages freedom of choice	93	88	97	93	113	107
Advocates the work ethic	81	90	101	94	94	125

*Only the left-hand phrase of the scale is shown. The smaller the mean or the larger the index value, the greater the agreement with the phrase.
**Index values significantly different at $p < .05$ using an F-test.

the image of younger individuals is consistent with their attitudes. Interestingly, these two groups tended to be in agreement for two attributes—high quality products and value for the money. They also possessed the most positive image of all the age groups for these two attributes.

Unlike attitudes, there are no significant differences in the image of capitalism with respect to level of education. Similarly, there is no relationship between perceptions of capitalism and household income.

Capitalism and Its Synonyms

Chapter 2 discussed differences in the definitions of capitalism and three other constructs often used to describe the American economic system—free enterprise, private enterprise, and American enterprise. It was found that the public's understanding and knowledge of capitalism are more vague and more abstract than its understanding and knowledge of the other constructs.

How do the images of these constructs compare and how do they relate to capitalism? Table 4.3 presents the mean values (and standard deviations) of each of the constructs for the thirteen attributes. There are statistically significant differences (p <.01) between at least two of the four constructs for all attributes except "allows political freedom," "produces high quality products," "promotes technology," and "leads to high living standard."

Across the attributes investigated, private enterprise was perceived the most positively. It was especially viewed as offering consumers good value for their money and promoting personal satisfaction. American enterprise was viewed the least favorably, especially with regard to "good value" and "personal satisfaction." In fact, private enterprise and American enterprise were perceived to differ significantly for seven of the thirteen attributes. Capitalism and American enterprise were generally perceived to possess slightly less positive images than either free enterprise or private enterprise.

Analogous to the results discussed in Chapter 2, on the basis of their respective standard deviations, there was more variability in perceptions of capitalism than exists for the remaining constructs. This finding also corroborates the previous conclusion that capitalism is a more vague and, perhaps, a less well understood and more complex construct than the others. On an absolute basis, though, all four constructs tended to be perceived as either possessing positive attributes or, as in the case of "inflationary tendency" and "growing in world prominence," being somewhat neutral.

To provide a "holistic" perspective on the image of capitalism and its synonyms, the constructs were "positioned" perceptually using the thirteen attributes simultaneously. This positioning resulted in the perceptual map in Figure 4.1.[4] The constructs are collectively represented by means of two functions or dimensions. These two dimensions consist of the attribute combinations that best differentiate among the constructs. The first is termed "political freedom and personal satisfaction" because these two attributes correlate with this dimension the strongest. The two attributes least relating to this dimension are "is dynamic" and "produces high quality products." The second is labelled "provides technology and is efficient" because of the attributes correlating most strongly with it. The two attributes least correlated with this dimension are "produces high quality products" and "offers consumers good value for their money." Of the two dimensions, the first is relatively more important in accounting for

Table 4.3 Perceptions of Capitalism and Its Synonyms

Attribute*	Mean (Standard Deviation)			
	Capitalism	Free enterprise	Private enterprise	American enterprise
Is inherently inflationary***	4.04(1.81)	3.91(1.82)	4.15(1.80)	3.64(1.72)
Is dynamic***	2.63(1.58)	2.55(1.39)	2.47(1.41)	2.91(1.53)
Is efficient in allocating resources***	3.43(1.72)	3.30(1.63)	3.23(1.52)	3.74(1.58)
Allows political freedom	2.79(1.85)	2.48(1.53)	2.47(1.48)	2.37(1.57)
Produces high quality products	3.04(1.68)	2.88(1.65)	2.73(1.53)	3.12(1.57)
Offers consumers good value for their money**	3.17(1.72)	2.95(1.58)	2.85(1.43)	3.47(1.62)
Is growing in world prominence**	3.73(1.76)	3.41(1.67)	3.36(1.72)	3.87(1.76)
Promotes personal satisfaction**	2.79(1.76)	2.46(1.49)	2.28(1.40)	2.95(1.57)
Is socially equitable***	3.44(1.76)	3.02(1.59)	3.00(1.57)	3.24(1.52)
Promotes technology	2.19(1.53)	2.10(1.22)	2.10(1.34)	2.39(1.40)
Leads to high living standard	2.52(1.73)	2.33(1.43)	2.38(1.36)	2.50(1.49)
Encourages freedom of choice***	2.51(1.78)	2.11(1.28)	2.08(1.24)	2.30(1.42)
Advocates the work ethic**	2.57(1.67)	2.33(1.31)	2.19(1.30)	2.73(1.57)

*Only the left-hand phrase of the scale is shown. The smaller the mean, the greater the agreement with the phrase.
**Means significantly different at $p<.001$ using an F-test.
***Means significantly different at $p<.01$ using an F-test.

differences in perceptions and hence should be accorded more "weight" when interpreting the perceptual map.

In one sense, the map summarizes the information contained in Table 4.3. Private enterprise appears to be perceived most positively, confirming the conclusion based on responses to the individual attributes. Capitalism is perceived as somewhat of an anomaly. Relative to the remaining constructs, it is perceived as allowing political freedom and personal satisfaction, but it is not perceived as promoting technology or efficiently allocating resources.

Capitalism, Socialism, and Communism

Since the American public does not appear to advocate replacing capitalism with a different system, it seems reasonable to hypothesize that the

Figure 4.1 Graphical Representation of Capitalism, Private Enterprise, American Enterprise, and Free Enterprise Perceptual Relationship

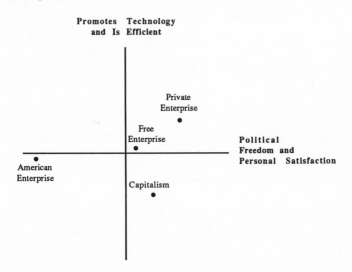

image of capitalism is more positive than the images of its major competitors, socialism and communism. This hypothesis was also tested by means of the benchmark sample.

The mean values and standard deviations for capitalism, socialism, and communism for each of the thirteen attributes are shown in Table 4.4. Comparing the three constructs through standard analyses of variance reveals that the public perceived the three very differently. Except for "growing in world prominence," all means differ significantly at $p<.001$. On an absolute basis, respondents reported being equally indifferent about the growth in world prominence of each of the three constructs.

With the exception of the view that it tends to be inherently inflationary, capitalism was viewed by the general public as possessing positive attributes whereas both socialism and communism were perceived as possessing negative attributes. In comparison with socialism and communism, capitalism was perceived especially as more dynamic, allowing political freedom, promoting personal satisfaction, leading to a high living standard, and encouraging freedom of choice. However, unlike the previous comparison of capitalism and related constructs, there are no consistently significant differences in the variability of perceptions of capitalism, socialism, and communism (on the basis of their respective standard deviations).

In general, the American public strongly distinguished between capitalism, socialism, and communism. With the exception of the

Table   4.4   Perceptions   of   Capitalism,   Socialism,   and Communism

Attribute*	Mean (Standard Deviation)		
	Capitalism	Socialism	Communism
Is inherently inflationary**	4.01(1.81)	4.29(1.86)	5.09(1.86)
Is dynamic**	2.63(1.58)	5.13(1.81)	5.86(1.63)
Is efficient in allocating resources**	3.43(1.72)	4.78(1.79)	5.50(1.77)
Allows political freedom**	2.79(1.85)	5.31(1.88)	6.64(1.04)
Produces high quality products**	3.04(1.68)	5.08(1.62)	5.47(1.67)
Offers consumers good value for their money**	3.17(1.72)	5.14(1.70)	5.89(1.50)
Is growing in world prominence	3.73(1.76)	3.64(1.77)	4.09(2.06)
Promotes personal satisfaction**	2.79(1.76)	5.39(1.69)	6.30(1.25)
Is socially equitable**	3.44(1.76)	5.08(1.78)	6.17(1.36)
Promotes technology**	2.19(1.53)	4.75(1.83)	4.82(1.99)
Leads to high living standard**	2.52(1.73)	5.39(1.67)	6.23(1.23)
Encourages freedom of choice**	2.51(1.78)	5.53(1.81)	6.63(.97)
Advocates the work ethic**	2.57(1.67)	4.85(2.02)	4.83(2.27)

*Only the left-hand phrase of the scale is shown. The smaller the mean, the greater the agreement with the phrase.
**Means significantly different at $p<.001$ using an F-test.

"inherently inflationary" attribute, communism was perceived more negatively than socialism.

As before, discriminant analysis of the thirteen attributes was used to produce a two-dimensional perceptual map of the three constructs. Figure 4.2 indicates that capitalism differed considerably from the other two constructs in the minds of the general public. Although both dimensions are statistically significant, the first function is more important in determining the configuration in the map. The two most important attributes in discriminating among the constructs for the first dimension are "encourages freedom of choice" and "leads to high living standard," whereas the two least important are "produces high quality products" and "promotes personal satisfaction." For the second dimension, the two most discriminating attributes are "allows political freedom" and "is socially equitable."

Figure 4.2   Graphic Representation of Capitalism, Socialism, and Communism Perceptual Relationship

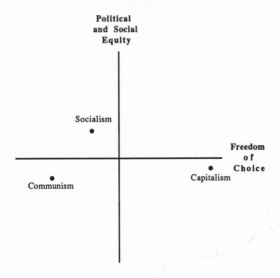

THE PERCEPTUAL RELATIONSHIP BETWEEN CAPITALISM AND BUSINESS

This section of the chapter extends the research on the image of capitalism by investigating the linkage between perceptions of capitalism and perceptions of business. Specifically, this section presents the results of investigating whether the public associates capitalism more with big business than it does with small business or all business.

As discussed previously, the public is typically thought of as being schizophrenic in its perception of business. Small business is often embraced as "good," whereas big business is considered "bad." Consequently, evidence on the accuracy of this perception is warranted.

In many regards, public perceptions of business parallel those of capitalism. Analogous to capitalism, business is not generally well understood by the public and there are differences in the perceptions of various subgroups. There is well-documented evidence that the public's view of business ebbs and flows with the economy.[5] Stated somewhat differently, the state of the economy strongly influences public perceptions of business. In times of prosperity, the public's opinion of business tends to be favorable; during recessions opinions become much more negative. Lipset has noted that public opinion toward business appears to be highly correlated with what he terms the "misery index," the sum of inflation and unemployment percentages.[6]

As mentioned in Chapter 3, it is important to make a distinction between the public's perception of business as an institution and its perception of business leaders. With a few exceptions, such as Chrysler chairman Lee Iacocca or Texas magnate Ross Perot, business leaders are frequently portrayed in the media as cheats, clowns, boorish, or uncaring.[7] Indeed, media coverage of the exploits and excesses of individuals such as Ivan Boesky, Malcolm Forbes, Leona Helmsley, Frank Lorenzo, Michael Milken, and Donald Trump tends to suggest business is generally corrupt and/or decadent. Moreover, one need only be exposed to motion pictures such as *Wall Street* or popular television programs such as *Dallas* to personally verify common business stereotypes. The investigation reported here focuses on the public's perception of business as an institution rather than its perception of business leaders.

The Data. In August 1987, a questionnaire was mailed to 1,600 households randomly selected from a national panel. One half of the questionnaires asked the male head of household to respond; the other half asked the female head to respond. In total, 998 responses were obtained for a response rate of 62 percent. To better reflect national population characteristics, sample data were weighted by gender and age using information from the Census Bureau. Consequently, the resulting sample represents middle-class adults possessing essentially the same characteristics as the benchmark sample.

The study employed a split-ballot approach. One half of the questionnaires inquired about the relationship between business and private enterprise. The other half inquired about the relationship between business and capitalism. The specific question posed was

Do you associate the word *private enterprise (capitalism)* with small business, big business, or all business?

A second split-ballot was overlaid with the first. One half of the questionnaires asked survey participants to respond to five semantic differential scales addressing characteristics of big business. The other half asked survey participants to respond to the same scales for small business. With one modification, these scales are those used in the benchmark study.[8]

Business Perceptions. Table 4.5 reveals a statistically significant relationship between the constructs capitalism/private enterprise and big/small business. Less than 4 percent of the general public associated capitalism only with small business, whereas 30 percent associated it only with big business. Simultaneously, 36 percent associated private enterprise with small business but only 10 percent associated it with big business. The no opinion percentages—22 percent for capitalism and 16 percent for

Table 4.5 **Perceived Relationship between Private Enterprise/Capitalism and Business**

	Percentage Response*			
Construct	Small business	Big business	All business	No opinion
Private enterprise	35.7	10.1	38.0	16.2
Capitalism	3.5	29.6	45.0	21.9

*Response distributions differ significantly at p<.001 using a χ^2 test.

private enterprise system—reinforce previous findings that as a construct, capitalism is not as well understood as private enterprise system. In brief, big business is generally associated with capitalism, whereas small business is associated with private enterprise.

Table 4.6 presents the results of comparing small with big business on five attributes. Figure 4.3 presents the same information shown in Table 4.6 in graphic form. As the table and figure show, small and big business were not perceived as differing in terms of being dynamic or stable, offering consumers good value for their money, or being the most efficient form of business. However, small business was perceived as producing significantly higher quality goods than big business. Simultaneously, though, big business was perceived as promoting technology more than small business.

In brief, the public viewed big business differently than it did small business. Interestingly enough, whereas big business is typically viewed as consisting of "Fortune 500-type" firms, there is no consensus on what constitutes small business. Perhaps the most widely used definition of small business is that of the Small Business Administration (SBA). This definition is based on Section 3 of the Small Business Act of 1953 (as amended):

> A small business concern shall be deemed to be one that is independently owned and operated and which is not dominant in its field of operation.

Quantitatively, the SBA's definition of a small business is a function of the industry in which it competes. Depending on the industry, the maximum number of employees a firm can have and still be classified by the SBA as a small business ranges from 500 to 1,500. The SBA sales volume standard ranges as high as $17 million.

Table 4.6   Public Perceptions of Big Business and Small Business

Attribute*	Mean (Standard Deviation)	
	Big Business	Small Business
Is dynamic	4.04 (1.47)	4.17 (1.35)
Produces low-quality goods**	4.30 (1.37)	5.30 (1.24)
Offers consumers good value for money	3.55 (1.41)	3.61 (1.51)
Promotes technology**	3.06 (1.61)	3.77 (1.52)
Least efficient form of business	4.49 (1.41)	4.57 (1.35)

*Only the left-hand phrase of the scale is shown. The smaller the mean, the greater the agreement with the phrase.
**Mean difference statistically significant at p<.001 using a t-test.

THE PUBLIC'S DEFINITION OF SMALL BUSINESS

In the mid-1980s, a study was conducted to determine how the general public defined "small business."[9] A four-page questionnaire was mailed to a random sample of 1,600 members of a national household panel. Of these questionnaires, 909 were returned for a response rate of 57 percent. The resulting data were weighted using 1984 Census Bureau information to arrive at a sample representative of middle-class adults.

Survey participants were asked three questions regarding the definition of a small business:

- What is your definition of a small business?
- Many definitions exist as to what is a small business. What do you think is the maximum number of full-time employees that a business can have and still be called a small business? _____ employees
- What are the maximum annual sales that a business can have and still be called a small business? $_____ sales

These questions addressed both the qualitative and quantitative dimensions of a definition of small business.

Content analysis of survey participants' definitions yielded nine primary dimensions and one "other" dimension. Approximately one-quarter of the survey participants could not provide any definition of a small

Figure 4.3   Public Perceptions of Big Business and Small Business

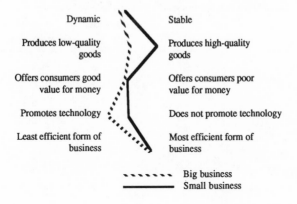

<table>
<tr><td>Dynamic</td><td>Stable</td></tr>
<tr><td>Produces low-quality goods</td><td>Produces high-quality goods</td></tr>
<tr><td>Offers consumers good value for money</td><td>Offers consumers poor value for money</td></tr>
<tr><td>Promotes technology</td><td>Does not promote technology</td></tr>
<tr><td>Least efficient form of business</td><td>Most efficient form of business</td></tr>
</table>

- - - - - - - Big business
————— Small business

business. Of those who did provide a definition, more than half, 56 percent, incorporated at least two different dimensions into their definitions.

Table 4.7 shows that the public's definition of a small business corresponds with the SBA definition, at least with respect to qualitative criteria. For example, the most frequent answer was "family owned"; 38 percent of the answers included this phrase. This response is similar to the SBA criterion of independent ownership. Likewise, the "small sales volume" response is consistent with the SBA criterion of no marketplace dominance. Of the survey participants incorporating two or more dimensions into their definitions, the most common combination was "a family-owned business with one outlet."

Quantitatively, however, the public's definition of small business and that of the SBA differ. The general public perceived small business in terms of so-called "mom and pop" businesses, particularly retail stores. In other words, the public's perception of a small business included only the smallest of the small. More than half of the surveyed individuals perceived a small business as having a maximum of ten employees. Likewise, more than half of the survey participants viewed a small business as having annual sales of less than $100,000. It may well be that the public's perception of small business was in large part derived from personal experience with very small retailers or from an idealistic perception of what a small business "should be."

Median responses to the number of employees and sales volume questions are contained in Table 4.8. The table reveals that in general:

- Males perceived a small business as being larger than did females.

Table 4.7   Major Dimensions of Small Business Definition

Dimension*	Percent of Sample Providing Dimension
Owner controls	3.3
Family-owned	38.4
One outlet	23.6
New business	2.0
Earns income/profit	7.4
Small sales volume	9.4
Small number of employees	13.2
Exact number of employees	15.5
Exact sales volume	5.9
Other	35.7

*A maximum of two responses was analyzed for each survey participant.

- The more education an individual possessed, the larger a small business was perceived to be.
- Individuals from households with annual incomes in excess of $20,000 perceived a small business as being larger than individuals from households with less than $20,000 incomes.
- The relationship between an individual's age and number of employees or sales volume was not statistically significant.

CONCLUSION

This chapter has investigated the public's image of capitalism and the linkage between perceptions of capitalism and business. Both the research reviewed and the research conducted lead to the same general conclusion. Compared with other constructs that are often used as synonyms for capitalism, perceptions of capitalism have greater variability in the minds of the American public. Capitalism is more vague, less understood, and more complex than the free enterprise system, the private enterprise system, or the American enterprise system.

The results of the research reported here suggest the American public (i.e., middle-class adults) perceives capitalism more positively than the alternatives of socialism and communism. At the same time, though, capitalism does not appear to possess the positive connotations that private enterprise does. The public tends to associate capitalism with big business,

Table 4.8   Median Number of Employees and Median Sales Volume of Small Business

| | Median Response | |
Characteristic	Number of Employees	Sales ($000)
Total Sample	10.2	$100.0
Gender*		
Male	12.5	$499.6
Female	10.0	99.8
Education*		
Less than high school degree	9.8	99.7
High school degree	9.9	100.1
Some college, trade or business school	10.4	200.2
College degree	19.7	499.5
Household income*		
Less than $20,000	9.9	99.7
$20,000 or more	11.7	250.0
Age		
Under 30	10.4	99.3
30-39	15.3	250.0
40-49	10.3	250.0
50-59	9.9	100.4
60 or older	10.1	160.5

*Number of employees and sales volume responses differ significantly by subgroup at $p<.001$ using an F-test.

whereas small business is associated with the private enterprise system. Although small business is viewed as producing higher quality goods than big business, big business is viewed as promoting technology more than small business. The latter perception is, at least in part, a function of the public's mental image of small business as consisting of "mom and pop" operations with very few employees and limited revenues.

NOTES

[1]David R. Gergen, "The Message to the Media, *Public Opinion,* Vol. 7 (April/May 1984): 6.

[2]Seymour M. Lipset and William Schneider, "How's Business? What the Public Thinks," *Public Opinion,* Vol. 1 (July/August 1978): 41-47.

[3]Analogous to the analysis of editor subgroups, a statistical significance criterion of $p < .05$ was employed because of small subgroup sample sizes.

[4]Mapping was accomplished by means of discriminant analysis, a commonly used multivariate technique that describes constructs (such as those investigated) in terms of underlying dimensions that differentiate or discriminate among them. Unlike analysis of variance in which each variable is investigated independently, discriminant analysis takes into account interrelationships among the variables being investigated.

[5]Burns W. Roper and Thomas A. W. Miller, "Americans Take Stock of Business," *Public Opinion,* Vol. 8 (August/September 1985): 12-15.

[6]Seymour M. Lipset, "Feeling Better: Measuring the Nation's Confidence," *Public Opinion,* Vol. 8 (April/May 1985): 6-9, 56ff.

[7]Ron Powers, "Businessmen Wear Black Hats," *Dun's Business Month,* Vol. 130 (December 1987): 70-74.

[8]Much of the material in this section has been drawn from Robert A. Peterson, Gerald Albaum, and George Kozmetsky, "Capitalism and Business: Public Perceptions," *Business Horizons,* Vol. 32 (May-June 1989): 63-66.

[9]See Robert A. Peterson, Gerald Albaum, and George Kozmetsky, "The Public's Definition of Small Business," *Journal of Small Business Management,* Vol. 24 (July 1986): 63-68.

5

Changes in Attitudes
toward Capitalism

Collectively, the previous chapters have documented the general public's understanding of, attitudes toward, and perceptions regarding capitalism. For the most part, the results reflect the state of knowledge and opinion in the early- to mid-1980s. For example, attitudes were measured at a time of relative economic euphoria. Ronald Reagan had just assumed the stewardship of the presidency and was extolling economic optimism—a return to the free market tenets of Adam Smith, lower income taxes, and less government regulation of business.

The 1980s were to prove tumultuous, both politically and economically. At the close of the decade the infrastructures of several communist nations literally exploded. Pressures for democratic principles and capitalism-based economies resounded throughout the USSR, Hungary, Romania, Bulgaria, Poland, and Czechoslovakia. Established governments were replaced, with the new governments embracing capitalism, oftentimes without thought about the consequences of such change.

However, at the same time capitalism was being praised throughout much of the world, events taking place in the United States may have reduced public confidence in it. Although there were no organized attacks on capitalism, *per se*, through the media, the efficacy of business and capitalism was more and more frequently being questioned, albeit rather indirectly. Events and activities involving individual companies and individual businesspeople, as well as business practices that were unusual, appear in retrospect to have led to increasing public mistrust of business in general.

The confluence of certain events and trends appears to have led to the restructuring of American industry. One such event was the effective restructuring of American industry and intensified competition due to the intrusion of foreign firms into the American marketplace. Firms from Japan and Korea, especially, made major competitive in-roads into automobiles and high-technology goods. An increasing number of elected officials and business leaders became economic xenophobes, and "Japan-bashing" was headline news.[1] Some individuals, though, believed the so-called "Japanese conspiracy" was nothing more than a hoax perpetrated on the American public.[2]

Simultaneously, American industry was being restructured through what have been termed "mega-mergers" and LBOs. In the mid-1980s, the use of so-called junk bonds to finance highly leveraged takeovers and acquisitions—both friendly and unfriendly—became rampant. Major companies such as Pillsbury and Nabisco were transformed virtually overnight, leading to fractious arguments regarding the impact of such mergers and financing on both the short-term health of the firms and the long-term viability of both the firms and the economy. By 1988, the consequences of some of the mergers and acquisitions came to the forefront when several highly visible takeovers (e.g., Campeau) resulted in questionable financial performance as well as bankruptcies.

A third form of industrial restructuring relates to the failure of numerous financial institutions. Literally hundreds of banks and savings and loan associations were forced to close their doors due to a combination of environmental and economic factors, mismanagement, and even fraudulent activities by corporate officials. These failures have, in turn, resulted in a massive government bail-out, a bail-out that will approximate a half trillion dollars—one-sixth of the annual federal government budget—and funded by taxpayer dollars.

Finally, during the latter half of the 1980s a resurgence of interest in entrepreneurship occurred, both in the private and the public sectors. According to some observers, entrepreneurial activities will lead to changes in the nature and structure of the economy during the 1990s.[3]

Restructuring has affected the life of virtually every American in one fashion or another. Consequently, it is logical to ask whether the attitudes of the general public toward capitalism have changed since the benchmarking study. Have the public's attitudes toward capitalism remained stable, or have they become more or less favorable? Similarly, have the attitudes of future leaders—college students—changed over the decade? To answer these questions, two studies were undertaken as the decade came to an end. The first was a follow-up of the general public study. The second was a follow-up study of college students (future leaders). The intent of both studies was twofold: to document current attitudes toward capitalism and compare these attitudes with those at the beginning of the 1980s. To facilitate these comparisons, virtually identical research methodologies were employed in the 1989 studies as in the 1980 studies.

WHAT THE PUBLIC THINKS: 1989

In late 1989, a questionnaire was mailed to a random sample of 2,250 households that were selected from a national panel. As in the benchmarking study, half of the questionnaires requested that the male head of household answer, whereas the other half requested that the female head of household answer. Survey participants were asked to respond to the same sixteen items used in the benchmarking study. Similar to the 1980 study, the data were weighted prior to analysis by gender and age to arrive at a sample that can be described as representing "middle-class adults" as of the end of 1989.

A total of 1,108 questionnaires was returned. This represents a 49 percent response rate. Responses were analyzed for survey participants as a group and for the demographic subgroups previously investigated—gender, age, education, household income, and marital status. In addition, specific comparisons were carried out between 1989 sample responses and 1980 sample responses.

Table 5.1 contains agreement percentages for the sixteen attitude items for both the 1980 and 1989 samples. The samples differ by more than 5 percentage points for ten of the items. In general, the responses suggest the general public in 1989 was slightly less positively disposed toward capitalism that it was in 1980. The largest difference occurs for the item "capitalism must be altered before any significant improvements in human welfare can be realized." A slight majority of the general public in 1989, 52 percent, agreed with this statement as compared with 38 percent in 1980. At the same time, a larger percentage of the general public (8 percentage points) in 1989 than in 1980 agreed that capitalism denies the masses property in life, liberty, and estate.

An interesting significant difference occurred for the item "capitalism is more than an economic system—it is a complex of institutions, attitudes, and cultures." Eighty-three percent of the general public in 1980 agreed with this statement as compared with 77 percent in 1989. This suggests that perhaps capitalism was viewed differently in 1989 than it was in 1980. It is possible that the general public viewed capitalism more simplistically in 1989 than it did in 1980.

In general, comparison of the 1980 and 1989 results reveals that there were more similarities in attitudes than dissimilarities, and attitudes were relatively more positive than negative. Even so, differences that occur are intriguing and warrant further investigation to provide insights into both the similarities and differences. Therefore, several analyses were undertaken. The first had as its purpose the examination of the attitudes of selected demographic subgroups.

Table 5.2 presents agreement percentages for five demographic variables.[4] Relative to the general public in 1980, in 1989 attitudes toward capitalism were more homogeneous. For example, in 1980 the attitudes of males differed significantly from those of females for fifteen of the sixteen items. In 1989, they differed for only two items. Likewise, in 1980 there were significant differences for eleven of the items across the age subgroups. In 1989 there were no significant differences among the age subgroups.

Table 5.1   Attitudes of the General Public toward Capitalism: 1980 and 1989

Attitude Item	Percentage Agreement	
	1980	1989
Capitalism denies the masses property in life, liberty, and estate.*	24.0	32.3
A capitalistic system advocates the work ethic and the free market mechanism.	81.6	80.6
A free society can exist under a capitalistic system.	77.3	73.4
Efficient management can only be achieved through capitalism.	57.4	53.9
Capitalists are entitled to the reward of profits because they assume the risk of loss.*	78.3	72.3
Capitalism is the most efficient economic system the world has ever known.*	68.0	61.3
Capitalism provides maximum benefits for society as a whole.*	66.4	59.0
Capitalism is more than an economic system—it is a complex of institutions, attitudes, and cultures.*	83.5	76.9
Capitalism basically relies on self-interest.	77.5	73.8
Capitalism provides people with personal incentives to make the most productive use of their assets.*	81.3	76.6
Capitalism must be altered before any significant improvements in human welfare can be realized.*	38.4	52.0
Capitalism encourages the efficient use of economic resources.*	66.1	59.9
The growth of the large corporation as the dominant form of business organization has endangered the existence of capitalism.	54.9	56.3
Capitalism encourages individual freedom of thought, choice, and action.*	76.9	71.2
In a capitalistic society, every individual has an opportunity to develop his/her own special abilities.*	76.3	69.3
Capitalism provides people with the highest living standard in the world.*	77.0	68.2

*Response difference statistically significant at p<.001 using a t-test on mean scale values.

Table 5.2   Attitudes of General Public toward Capitalism by Gender, Age, Education, Income, and Marital Status: 1989

Attitude Item	Percentage Agreement Gender	
	Male	Female
Capitalism denies the masses property in life, liberty, and estate.*	27.1	37.0
A capitalistic system advocates the work ethic and the free market mechanism.	80.8	80.5
A free society can exist under a capitalistic system.*	77.5	69.8
Efficient management can only be achieved through capitalism.	58.1	50.2
Capitalists are entitled to the reward of profits because they assume the risk of loss.	74.1	70.6
Capitalism is the most efficient economic system the world has ever known.	62.1	60.6
Capitalism provides maximum benefits for society as a whole.	59.4	58.5
Capitalism is more than an economic system—it is a complex of institutions, attitudes, and cultures.	76.6	77.2
Capitalism basically relies on self-interest.	76.9	71.0
Capitalism provides people with personal incentives to make the most productive use of their assets.	78.0	75.3
Capitalism must be altered before any significant improvements in human welfare can be realized.	51.5	52.5
Capitalism encourages the efficient use of economic resources.	61.2	58.8
The growth of the large corporation as the dominant form of business organization has endangered the existence of capitalism.	56.1	56.5
Capitalism encourages individual freedom of thought, choice, and action.	73.3	69.3
In a capitalistic society, every individual has an opportunity to develop his/her own special abilities.	70.3	68.3
Capitalism provides people with the highest living standard in the world.	70.6	66.0

Table 5.2 (continued)

Attitude Item	Percentage Agreement Age				
	25-34	35-44	45-54	55-64	65 and over
Capitalism denies the masses property in life, liberty, and estate.	36.2	29.2	32.2	28.3	33.4
A capitalistic system advocates the work ethic and the free market mechanism.	86.4	78.6	81.3	79.0	75.2
A free society can exist under a capitalistic system.	73.5	74.8	75.3	75.3	68.8
Efficient management can only be achieved through capitalism.	52.8	52.9	54.7	57.4	53.7
Capitalists are entitled to the reward of profits because they assume the risk of loss.	72.4	72.9	73.3	75.3	68.1
Capitalism is the most efficient economic system the world has ever known.	57.6	61.0	61.5	67.8	62.2
Capitalism provides maximum benefits for society as a whole.	55.3	61.1	58.2	65.5	57.7
Capitalism is more than an economic system— it is a complex of institutions, attitudes, and cultures.	75.8	79.9	79.8	77.6	72.3
Capitalism basically relies on self-interest.	77.2	77.7	76.3	70.3	64.9
Capitalism provides people with personal incentives to make the most productive use of their assets.	76.4	78.1	74.6	76.5	76.7
Capitalism must be altered before any significant improvements in human welfare can be realized.	56.3	50.8	51.6	44.1	53.3
Capitalism encourages the efficient use of economic resources.	57.1	56.1	62.7	63.9	63.5
The growth of the large corporation as the dominant form of business organization has endangered the existence of capitalism.	55.2	52.5	63.4	61.3	53.1
Capitalism encourages individual freedom of thought, choice, and action.	70.1	74.3	70.5	71.8	69.5
In a capitalistic society, every individual has an opportunity to develop his/her own special abilities.	69.6	68.7	68.7	72.5	67.5
Capitalism provides people with the highest living standard in the world.	62.4	73.0	69.0	72.9	66.9

Table 5.2 (continued)

Attitude Item	Percentage Agreement Education Level			
	Less than high school	High school	Some college	College graduate
Capitalism denies the masses property in life, liberty, and estate.*	55.6	44.1	29.5	14.4
A capitalistic system advocates the work ethic and the free market mechanism.	77.1	77.8	83.0	84.4
A free society can exist under a capitalistic system.*	64.1	67.2	76.5	81.3
Efficient management can only be achieved through capitalism.	54.7	52.2	49.9	60.2
Capitalists are entitled to the reward of profits because they assume the risk of loss.*	58.1	68.4	75.5	78.6
Capitalism is the most efficient economic system the world has ever known.	53.9	56.9	65.9	65.5
Capitalism provides maximum benefits for society as a whole.*	45.8	55.6	62.5	64.6
Capitalism is more than an economic system—it is a complex of institutions, attitudes, and cultures.*	67.7	73.0	78.9	83.8
Capitalism basically relies on self-interest.*	74.0	66.1	79.9	79.3
Capitalism provides people with personal incentives to make the most productive use of their assets.*	68.0	70.3	79.1	84.1
Capitalism must be altered before any significant improvements in human welfare can be realized.*	67.2	53.7	52.5	44.0
Capitalism encourages the efficient use of economic resources.	50.8	59.5	60.3	62.3
The growth of the large corporation as the dominant form of business organization has endangered the existence of capitalism.	60.0	55.1	60.6	51.1
Capitalism encourages individual freedom of thought, choice, and action.	66.0	69.5	72.1	75.3
In a capitalistic society, every individual has an opportunity to develop his/her own special abilities.	60.6	68.3	72.3	70.5
Capitalism provides people with the highest living standard in the world.*	59.3	65.6	69.9	74.3

Table 5.2 (continued)

Attitude Item	Percentage Agreement Income			
	Under $12,500	$12,500-$22,499	$22,500-$40,000	$40,000 or more
Capitalism denies the masses property in life, liberty, and estate.	47.3	57.6	60.1	65.7
A capitalistic system advocates the work ethic and the free market mechanism.*	65.3	69.9	82.6	82.6
A free society can exist under a capitalistic system.	67.3	71.8	75.9	74.6
Efficient management can only be achieved through capitalism.*	69.5	73.7	81.1	79.3
Capitalists are entitled to the reward of profits because they assume the risk of loss.	57.1	54.6	51.8	47.4
Capitalism is the most efficient economic system the world has ever known.	63.9	53.9	63.3	60.9
Capitalism provides maximum benefits for society as a whole.	60.8	56.1	56.7	54.6
Capitalism is more than an economic system—it is a complex of institutions, attitudes, and cultures.*	67.3	64.0	72.6	76.0
Capitalism basically relies on self-interest.	63.5	66.5	70.6	72.2
Capitalism provides people with personal incentives to make the most productive use of their assets.*	60.6	62.7	69.9	74.6
Capitalism must be altered before any significant improvements in human welfare can be realized.	39.5	38.8	42.0	38.9
Capitalism encourages the efficient use of economic resources.*	27.2	16.2	11.9	14.3
The growth of the large corporation as the dominant form of business organization has endangered the existence of capitalism.	73.0	78.4	78.8	74.4
Capitalism encourages individual freedom of thought, choice, and action.*	63.3	60.0	62.9	50.4
In a capitalistic society, every individual has an opportunity to develop his/her own special abilities.*	49.7	54.8	65.0	61.9
Capitalism provides people with the highest living standard in the world.	50.8	58.2	66.2	61.2

Table 5.2 (continued)

Attitude Item	Percentage Agreement Marital Status		
	Married	Never married	Other
Capitalism denies the masses property in life, liberty, and estate.	31.8	25.0	40.1
A capitalistic system advocates the work ethic and the free market mechanism.*	82.4	84.2	72.3
A free society can exist under a capitalistic system.	74.4	77.9	66.8
Efficient management can only be achieved through capitalism.	54.6	53.9	51.9
Capitalists are entitled to the reward of profits because they assume the risk of loss.	74.0	75.1	64.4
Capitalism is the most efficient economic system the world has ever known.	63.0	58.5	58.3
Capitalism provides maximum benefits for society as a whole.	61.4	58.3	51.6
Capitalism is more than an economic system—it is a complex of institutions, attitudes, and cultures.	80.1	70.2	72.4
Capitalism basically relies on self-interest.	75.3	77.7	66.2
Capitalism provides people with personal incentives to make the most productive use of their assets.	77.4	77.8	73.1
Capitalism must be altered before any significant improvements in human welfare can be realized.	50.3	49.8	59.2
Capitalism encourages the efficient use of economic resources.	61.6	55.5	58.2
The growth of the large corporation as the dominant form of business organization has endangered the existence of capitalism.	58.2	55.6	50.9
Capitalism encourages individual freedom of thought, choice, and action.	72.3	73.2	66.2
In a capitalistic society, every individual has an opportunity to develop his/her own special abilities.	71.1	68.3	64.2
Capitalism provides people with the highest living standard in the world.	71.5	65.6	59.6

*Responses significantly different at $p < .001$ using an F-test.

The only demographic characteristic for which the pattern of differences observed in 1980 was continued in 1989 was education. Analogous to 1980, individuals with more education tended to be more positively disposed toward capitalism than were individuals with less education. More specifically, individuals with less than a high school degree were the least favorably disposed toward capitalism, whereas individuals with a college degree were the most favorably disposed toward it. Moreover, the differences between these two demographic subgroups has grown larger over the decade. To illustrate, in 1989 approximately two-thirds of the individuals with less than a high school degree believed that capitalism must be altered before any improvements in human welfare can be realized. Simultaneously, only 44 percent of the individuals with a college degree or more hold this belief, a difference of 23 percentage points.

It is not possible to explain precisely why changes occurred in the general public's attitude between 1980 and 1989. However, it is possible to make certain inferences as to whether there were wholesale shifts in attitudes, whether the shifts were only for specific segments of the public, or whether the observed shifts merely reflected a changing public composition. With respect to the latter, for example, to the extent the public differed demographically at the times attitudes were measured, this would possibly lead to differences in attitudes. However, a comparison of the demographic characteristics of the two samples suggests they are comparable. To the extent they differ, the differences reflect general societal changes that occurred over the decade.

Table 5.3 presents differences in agreement percentages for each of the sixteen items for four of the demographic subgroups analyzed. Because the household incomes over the study period are not strictly comparable, no attempt was made to assess attitude differences for this characteristic. A positive difference in the table signifies that the 1989 agreement response percentage was larger than the 1980 agreement response percentage. Consider the first statement, "Capitalism denies the masses property, life, liberty, and estate." Ten percent more males agreed with this statement in 1989 than in 1980, whereas 5 percent more females agreed with it in 1989 than in 1980. Table 5.4 shows the average absolute difference in agreement percentages for each of the demographic subgroups.[5] The table reveals that the largest difference in agreement percentages occurred for males, whereas the smallest difference in agreement percentages occurred for females.

Together, Tables 5.3 and 5.4 indicate that the attitude changes evinced from 1980 to 1989 were effectively driven by changes in attitudes held by males. In 1989 males were considerably more skeptical of capitalism than they were in 1980. Indeed, in 1989 their responses were very similar to those of females, who were relatively less positive toward capitalism than males in 1980. Female attitudes appear to be relatively stable. There are no significant differences between the agreement responses of females in 1980 and 1989.

Table 5.3   1980-1989 Attitude Changes of General Public toward Capitalism

Attitude Item	Percentage Change Gender	
	Male	Female
Capitalism denies the masses property in life, liberty, and estate.	+10.1*	+4.7
A capitalistic system advocates the work ethic and the free market mechanism.	-6.0*	+5.0
A free society can exist under a capitalistic system.	-7.1*	+.5
Efficient management can only be achieved through capitalism.	-4.2	-1.9
Capitalists are entitled to the reward of profits because they assume the risk of loss.	-11.7*	+1.0
Capitalism is the most efficient economic system the world has ever known.	-12.2*	0.0
Capitalism provides maximum benefits for society as a whole.	-10.0*	-3.5
Capitalism is more than an economic system—it is a complex of institutions, attitudes, and cultures.	-11.1*	-1.8
Capitalism basically relies on self-interest.	-4.2	-1.7
Capitalism provides people with personal incentives to make the most productive use of their assets.	-9.7*	+.5
Capitalism must be altered before any significant improvements in human welfare can be realized.	+20.5*	-5.4
Capitalism encourages the efficient use of economic resources.	-7.5*	-3.6
The growth of the large corporation as the dominant form of business organization has endangered the existence of capitalism.	+2.9	0.0
Capitalism encourages individual freedom of thought, choice, and action.	-10.0*	-1.1
In a capitalistic society, every individual has an opportunity to develop his/her own special abilities.	-12.6*	-1.8
Capitalism provides people with the highest living standard in the world.	-12.7*	-3.7

Table 5.3 (continued)

Attitude Item	Percentage Change Age				
	25-34	35-44	45-54	55-64	65 and over
Capitalism denies the masses property in life, liberty, and estate.	+11.2	+4.0	+15.3*	-.1	+3.0
A capitalistic system advocates the work ethic and the free market mechanism.	+6.0	-3.1	-5.2	-1.2	-1.1
A free society can exist under a capitalistic system.	-2.2	-.8	-6.7	+.3	-5.4
Efficient management can only be achieved through capitalism.	+1.8	-1.3	-10.3	-1.3	-5.8
Capitalists are entitled to the reward of profits because they assume the risk of loss.	-6.4	-3.2	-7.2	+1.8	-7.4
Capitalism is the most efficient economic system the world has ever known.	-4.3	-1.8	-10.8	-1.9	-8.4
Capitalism provides maximum benefits for society as a whole.	-6.6	-3.5	-14.8*	+.1	-10.6
Capitalism is more than an economic system—it is a complex of institutions, attitudes, and cultures.	-7.8	-4.2	-4.6	-5.2	-6.6
Capitalism basically relies on self-interest.	-.8	-.3	-.6	-8.3	-6.4
Capitalism provides people with personal incentives to make the most productive use of their assets.	-2.6	-3.9	-9.0	-3.9	-1.8
Capitalism must be altered before any significant improvements in human welfare can be realized.	+18.0*	+8.5*	+17.8*	+3.7	+8.5
Capitalism encourages the efficient use of economic resources.	-3.9	-6.4	-6.9	-3.9	-7.5
The growth of the large corporation as the dominant form of business organization has endangered the existence of capitalism.	+1.1	+1.0	+5.8	+9.2	+1.0
Capitalism encourages individual freedom of thought, choice, and action.	-4.8	-.3	-11.1	-5.1	-4.9
In a capitalistic society, every individual has an opportunity to develop his/her own special abilities.	-5.1	-3.7	-10.7	-3.6	-7.8
Capitalism provides people with the highest living standard in the world.	-10.6	-3.3	-11.4	-4.1	-9.1

Table 5.3 (continued)

Attitude Item	Percentage Change Education Level			
	Less than high school	High school	Some college	College graduate
Capitalism denies the masses property in life, liberty, and estate.	+13.8	+13.2	+7.6	-3.9
A capitalistic system advocates the work ethic and the free market mechanism.	+14.2	+2.7	-2.1	-2.5
A free society can exist under a capitalistic system.	+5.7	-2.6	-2.1	-3.8
Efficient management can only be achieved through capitalism.	+8.2	+1.2	-11.2	-1.9
Capitalists are entitled to the reward of profits because they assume the risk of loss.	+3.8	-1.9	-2.7	-6.4
Capitalism is the most efficient economic system the world has ever known.	-1.0	-3.8	-7.3	-4.2
Capitalism provides maximum benefits for society as a whole.	-12.0	-6.4	-6.5	-2.9
Capitalism is more than an economic system—it is a complex of institutions, attitudes, and cultures.	-3.8	-5.9	-5.6	-5.2*
Capitalism basically relies on self-interest.	+2.8	-5.1	+1.8	-2.2
Capitalism provides people with personal incentives to make the most productive use of their assets.	-.6	-5.6	-3.7	-2.7
Capitalism must be altered before any significant improvements in human welfare can be realized.	+17.4	+7.5	+12.8*	+11.6*
Capitalism encourages the efficient use of economic resources.	-12.2*	-.9	-6.5	-6.8
The growth of the large corporation as the dominant form of business organization has endangered the existence of capitalism.	+6.8	-.9	+4.8	-2.9
Capitalism encourages individual freedom of thought, choice, and action.	+1.5	+.2	-8.9	-6.9
In a capitalistic society, every individual has an opportunity to develop his/her own special abilities.	-1.2	-2.9	-9.1	-8.7
Capitalism provides people with the highest living standard in the world.	-1.0	-4.5	-10.2*	-8.3

Table 5.3 (continued)

Attitude Item	Percentage Agreement Marital Status		
	Married	Never Married	Other
Capitalism denies the masses property in life, liberty, and estate.	+3.6	+5.0	+8.4
A capitalistic system advocates the work ethic and the free market mechanism.	+2.1	-4.2	-2.3
A free society can exist under a capitalistic system.	-.2	-6.9	-6.8
Efficient management can only be achieved through capitalism.	-3.2	-2.5	-.3
Capitalists are entitled to the reward of profits because they assume the risk of loss.	-1.9	-8.6	-7.6
Capitalism is the most efficient economic system the world has ever known.	-4.4	-5.4	-5.5
Capitalism provides maximum benefits for society as a whole.	-5.6	-5.8	-8.6
Capitalism is more than an economic system—it is a complex of institutions, attitudes, and cultures.	-7.1	-8.9*	-10.4*
Capitalism basically relies on self-interest.	+.2	-5.1	-8.0
Capitalism provides people with personal incentives to make the most productive use of their assets.	-3.1	-6.6	-3.4
Capitalism must be altered before any significant improvements in human welfare can be realized.	+9.1*	+14.4	+16.2
Capitalism encourages the efficient use of economic resources.	-4.1	-12.0	+3.1
The growth of the large corporation as the dominant form of business organization has endangered the existence of capitalism.	+1.3	+4.1	-1.2
Capitalism encourages individual freedom of thought, choice, and action.	-2.7	-9.6	-7.5
In a capitalistic society, every individual has an opportunity to develop his/her own special abilities.	-4.3	-8.9	-9.2
Capitalism provides people with the highest living standard in the world.	-4.1	-13.9*	-12.6

*1980-1989 difference statistically significant at p<.001 using a t-test on mean scale values.

Table 5.4 **Average** **Absolute** **Differences** **in** **Agreement** **Percentages:** **1980-1989**

Subgroup	Average Absolute Difference
Gender	
Male	9.5
Female	2.3
Age	
25-34	5.8
35-44	3.1
45-54	9.3
55-64	3.4
65 and older	6.0
Education	
Less than high school degree	6.6
High school graduate	4.1
Some college or trade school	6.4
College graduate	5.1
Marital Status	
Married	3.6
Never married	7.6
Other (widowed, etc.)	6.9

The second largest change in agreement percentages occurred for the age group 45-54. Overall, this particular age group, which previously was relatively disposed toward capitalism, exhibited relatively fewer positive attitudes toward capitalism in 1989. To provide further insights into this finding, a cohort analysis was undertaken.[6]

A cohort is a group of individuals who have experienced a common significant life event (in most instances the significant life event is birth in a particular time period, usually in a specific decade). Cohort analysis is an approach for analyzing changes or shifts over time when longitudinal data are not available. To carry out a cohort analysis, it is necessary that the age group encompassed by the cohort correspond to the time period being investigated. In the present instance, three cohorts were studied: individuals 25-34 years of age in 1980, individuals 35-44 years of age in 1980, and individuals 45-54 years of age in 1980. Responses of the former in 1980 were compared with those of individuals 35-44 in 1989, those of the latter compared with individuals 55-64 in 1989, and so forth. The intent is to draw, wherever possible, conclusions about whether the attitudes held in 1989 reflect changes due to environmental occurrences, aging, or some other factor.

Results of the cohort analysis are reported in Table 5.5. For the most part, cohort changes were in the direction of less positive attitudes toward capitalism. From the table it appears that attitude change relates to aging. As shown below, the older an individual, the greater the attitude change.

1980 age cohort	*Average absolute difference*
25-34	2.9
35-44	4.3
45-54	7.2

To further facilitate the interpretation of the public's attitudes toward capitalism, agreement percentages in the two studies were compared with those obtained in a 1987 study of the general public. In the 1987 study, the same basic research methodology—a questionnaire mailed to a representative sample of a national panel—was employed (see Chapter 4). In 1987, however, only five of the sixteen attitude items were included in the study. Table 5.6 presents these items as well as the agreement percentages for each of the three years. The agreement percentages indicate that the decrease in positive attitudes toward capitalism revealed in the 1989 study has resulted primarily since 1987. The percentages also corroborate what was suggested previously. It may well be that in 1989 the general public perceived capitalism as more limited in scope than it did in either 1980 or 1987. Finally, the percentages suggest the potential impact of study timing on public attitudes. That is, attitudes may be influenced by momentary occurrences (e.g., the events previously discussed) that artificially inflate or deflate measurements of them.

Finally, responses to the sixteen attitudinal items were factor-analyzed to assess whether structural changes in attitudes had occurred between 1980 and 1989. Factor analysis of the 1980 data in Chapter 3 indicated a single factor accounted for the underlying attitudinal structure. Comparison of the 1980 factor structure with the 1989 factor structure revealed the structures were virtually identical. In other words, although the "level" or "intensity" of attitudes may have changed somewhat over the time period, the underlying attitudinal structure was essentially constant.

Table 5.5 Cohort Analysis of Attitudes toward Capitalism

Attitude Item	Percentage Agreement Age		
	1980 25-34	1989 35-44	Change
Capitalism denies the masses property in life, liberty, and estate.	25.0	29.2	+4.2
A capitalistic system advocates the work ethic and the free market mechanism.	80.4	78.6	-1.8
A free society can exist under a capitalistic system.	75.7	74.8	-.9
Efficient management can only be achieved through capitalism.	51.0	52.9	+1.9
Capitalists are entitled to the reward of profits because they assume the risk of loss.	78.0	72.9	-5.1
Capitalism is the most efficient economic system the world has ever known.	61.9	61.0	-.9
Capitalism provides maximum benefits for society as a whole.	61.9	61.6	-.3
Capitalism is more than an economic system—it is a complex of institutions, attitudes, and cultures.	83.6	79.9	-3.7
Capitalism basically relies on self-interest.	78.0	77.7	-.3
Capitalism provides people with personal incentives to make the most productive use of their assets.	79.0	78.1	-.9
Capitalism must be altered before any significant improvements in human welfare can be realized.*	38.3	50.8	+12.5
Capitalism encourages the efficient use of economic resources.	61.0	56.1	-4.9
The growth of the large corporation as the dominant form of business organization has endangered the existence of capitalism.	54.1	52.5	-1.6
Capitalism encourages individual freedom of thought, choice, and action.	74.9	74.3	-.6
In a capitalistic society, every individual has an opportunity to develop his/her own special abilities.	74.7	68.7	-6.0
Capitalism provides people with the highest living standard in the world.	73.0	73.0	0.0

Table 5.5 (continued)

Attitude Item	Percentage Agreement Age		
	1980 35-44	1989 45-54	Change
Capitalism denies the masses property in life, liberty, and estate.	25.2	32.2	+7.0
A capitalistic system advocates the work ethic and the free market mechanism.	81.7	81.3	-.4
A free society can exist under a capitalistic system.	75.6	75.3	-.3
Efficient management can only be achieved through capitalism.	54.2	54.7	+.5
Capitalists are entitled to the reward of profits because they assume the risk of loss.	76.1	73.3	-2.8
Capitalism is the most efficient economic system the world has ever known.	62.8	61.5	-1.3
Capitalism provides maximum benefits for society as a whole.	64.6	58.2	-6.4
Capitalism is more than an economic system—it is a complex of institutions, attitudes, and cultures.	84.1	79.8	-4.3
Capitalism basically relies on self-interest.	78.0	76.3	-1.7
Capitalism provides people with personal incentives to make the most productive use of their assets.	82.0	74.6	-7.4
Capitalism must be altered before any significant improvements in human welfare can be realized.*	42.3	51.6	+9.3
Capitalism encourages the efficient use of economic resources.	62.5	62.7	+.2
The growth of the large corporation as the dominant form of business organization has endangered the existence of capitalism.*	51.5	63.4	+11.9
Capitalism encourages individual freedom of thought, choice, and action.	74.6	70.5	-4.1
In a capitalistic society, every individual has an opportunity to develop his/her own special abilities.	72.4	68.7	-3.7
Capitalism provides people with the highest living standard in the world.	76.3	69.0	-7.3

Table 5.5 (continued)

Attitude Item	Percentage Agreement Age		
	1980 45-54	1989 55-64	Change
Capitalism denies the masses property in life, liberty, and estate.*	16.9	28.3	+11.4
A capitalistic system advocates the work ethic and the free market mechanism.	86.5	79.0	-7.5
A free society can exist under a capitalistic system.	82.0	75.3	-6.7
Efficient management can only be achieved through capitalism.	65.0	57.4	-7.6
Capitalists are entitled to the reward of profits because they assume the risk of loss.	80.5	75.3	-5.2
Capitalism is the most efficient economic system the world has ever known.	72.3	67.8	-4.5
Capitalism provides maximum benefits for society as a whole.	73.0	65.5	-7.5
Capitalism is more than an economic system—it is a complex of institutions, attitudes, and cultures.	84.4	77.6	-6.8
Capitalism basically relies on self-interest.	76.9	70.3	-6.6
Capitalism provides people with personal incentives to make the most productive use of their assets.	83.6	76.5	-7.1
Capitalism must be altered before any significant improvements in human welfare can be realized.*	33.8	44.1	+10.3
Capitalism encourages the efficient use of economic resources.	69.6	63.9	-5.7
The growth of the large corporation as the dominant form of business organization has endangered the existence of capitalism.	57.6	61.3	+3.7
Capitalism encourages individual freedom of thought, choice, and action.	81.6	71.8	-9.8
In a capitalistic society, every individual has an opportunity to develop his/her own special abilities.	79.4	72.5	-6.9
Capitalism provides people with the highest living standard in the world.	80.4	72.9	-7.5

*Difference significant at p<.01 using a t-test on mean scale values.

Table 5.6   Public Attitudes toward Capitalism: 1980, 1987, and 1989

Attitude Item	Percentage Agreement		
	1980	1987	1989
Capitalism is the most efficient economic system the world has ever known.*	68.0	72.5	61.3
Capitalism provides maximum benefits for society as a whole.*	66.4	66.5	59.0
Capitalism is more than an economic system—it is a complex of institutions, attitudes, and cultures.*	83.5	82.7	76.9
Capitalism encourages the efficient use of economic resources.	66.1	66.4	59.9
Capitalism provides people with the highest living standard in the world.*	77.0	69.2	68.2

*Differences statistically significant at $p < .001$ using an F-test.

COLLEGE STUDENT ATTITUDES

In the fall of 1989, a survey was conducted to determine whether the attitudes of future leaders (college students) had changed from the 1980 study. Questionnaires were administered to undergraduate students attending a random sample of sixteen of the twenty-eight universities surveyed in the 1980 study. As before, both public and private institutions were included in the sample. A total of 1,681 completed questionnaires was obtained from the follow-up survey. The resulting data were again weighted by means of Census Bureau statistics to reflect university enrollments in three general fields of study—business, liberal arts or social sciences, and engineering or natural sciences. Analogous to the initial study, five attitude items were investigated.

As Table 5.7 shows, college students in 1989 were somewhat more favorable toward capitalism than were college students in 1980. Agreement percentages differed significantly for three of the five items. The largest difference occurred for the item "capitalists are entitled to the reward of

Table 5.7 Attitudes of College Students toward Capitalism: 1980 and 1989

Attitude Item	Percentage Agreement	
	1980	1989
Capitalism denies the masses property in life, liberty, and estate.	36.3	34.6
A capitalistic system advocates the work ethic and the free market mechanism.*	71.9	75.5
A free society can exist under a capitalistic system.	70.8	75.1
Efficient management can only be achieved through capitalism.*	47.9	53.1
Capitalists are entitled to the reward of profits because they assume the risk of loss.*	65.6	75.9

*Response difference is statistically significant at $p<.001$ using a t-test on mean scale values.

profits because they assume the risk of loss." Whereas 66 percent of the students in 1980 agreed with this item, 76 percent agreed with it in 1989.

Table 5.8 reports agreement percentages by college student gender, major, and academic classification. The results are relatively consistent with those obtained in the benchmark student study. Males were more favorable toward capitalism than were females, and business majors tended to be more favorable than were nonbusiness majors. However, unlike the benchmark study, agreement percentages did not differ by academic classification.

Table 5.9 presents agreement percentage differences between the 1980 and 1989 samples of college students. As shown below, the largest changes in attitudes occurred for freshmen, whereas the smallest occurred for engineering or natural science majors.

Finally, a comparison of attitudes toward capitalism held by college students and the general public is shown in Table 5.10. The table demonstrates how the attitudes of college students have changed over the past decade. Whereas their attitudes were less positive than those of the general public in 1980, they were as positive or more positive in 1989.

Table 5.8 Attitudes of College Students toward Capitalism by Gender, Major, and Academic Classification: 1989

| | Percentage Agreement | | | | |
| | Gender | | Major | | |
Attitude Item	Male	Female	Bus-iness	Liberal arts	Engin-eering
Capitalism denies the masses property in life, liberty, and estate.	29.8*	35.8	26.7*	37.1	35.8
A capitalistic system advocates the work ethic and the free market mechanism.	79.6*	74.1	80.4	74.8	73.3
A free society can exist under a capitalistic system.	81.9*	70.8	81.2*	73.2	72.7
Efficient management can only be achieved through capitalism.	57.6*	50.7	58.1	50.7	52.4
Capitalists are entitled to the reward of profits because they assume the risk of loss.	83.0*	73.4	85.0*	72.0	75.3

Student group	*Average absolute difference in percent agreement: 1980-1989*
Gender	
Male	4.6
Female	4.8
Major	
Business	6.0
Liberal Arts	5.1
Engineering	3.3
Classification	
Freshman	11.9
Sophomore	6.3
Junior	3.4
Senior	3.8

Table 5.8 (continued)

| Attitude Item | Percentage Agreement Academic Classification | | | |
	Freshman	Sophomore	Junior	Senior
Capitalism denies the masses property in life, liberty, and estate.	30.7	27.1	36.5	32.0
A capitalistic system advocates the work ethic and the free market mechanism.	73.7	77.3	74.0	78.4
A free society can exist under a capitalistic system.	73.8	78.5	73.8	77.9
Efficient management can only be achieved through capitalism.	58.1	52.5	52.4	55.7
Capitalists are entitled to the reward of profits because they assume the risk of loss.	79.8	78.2	76.9	79.2

*Response difference is statistically significant at $p < .001$ using an F-test.

Although it is not possible to know exactly *why* differences in attitudes exist between the two samples, differences are no doubt due, in part, to two trends. The first is that relatively more students are enrolled in business curricula in 1989 than in 1980. According to the *Statistical Abstract of the United States,* 20 percent of the college degrees conferred in 1980 were in business. By 1986, this percentage had risen to 25 percent. Hence, given the relationship between major (academic field) and attitudes toward capitalism and the increase in business majors, the differences observed in the two sets of agreement percentages are both intuitively logical and consistent with expectations. If this educational trend continues, one would expect the attitudes of college students toward capitalism to become slightly more favorable in the 1990s. Second, studies of college students have documented trends toward more conservative life styles and attitudes in the latter half of the 1980s. Such trends are consistent with the findings in the 1989 study.

Table 5.9   Attitude Changes of College Students toward Capitalism

Attitude Item	Percentage Change				
	Gender		Major		
	Male	Female	Business	Liberal arts	Engineering
Capitalism denies the masses property in life, liberty, and estate.	-2.3	-0.0	-3.3	-.4	-2.0
A capitalistic system advocates the work ethic and the free market mechanism.	+3.5	+2.9	+3.7	+5.3	+.3
A free society can exist under a capitalistic system.	+3.4	+5.2	+6.3*	+5.1	-1.0
Efficient management can only be achieved through capitalism.	+5.3	+5.3	+6.9*	+5.4	+2.2
Capitalists are entitled to the reward of profits because they assume the risk of loss.	+8.4*	+10.4*	+9.6*	+9.3*	+11.2

Attitude Item	Percentage Change			
	Academic Classification			
	Freshman	Sophomore	Junior	Senior
Capitalism denies the masses property in life, liberty, and estate.	-7.1	-10.9	+2.5	-.1
A capitalistic system advocates the work ethic and the free market mechanism.	+4.6	+5.3	0.0	+3.3
A free society can exist under a capitalistic system.	+11.3	+3.6	+2.0	+3.4
Efficient management can only be achieved through capitalism.	+16.3*	+1.1	+4.1	+4.7
Capitalists are entitled to the reward of profits because they assume the risk of loss.	+20.3*	+10.8*	+8.4*	+7.4*

*Response difference is statistically significant at $p<.001$ using a t-test on mean scale values.

Table 5.10   Attitude Comparison between the General Public and College Students: 1980 and 1989

Attitude Item	Percentage Agreement 1980		1989	
	General public	College students	General public	College students
Capitalism denies the masses property in life, liberty, and estate.	24.0	36.3	32.3	34.6
A capitalistic system advocates the work ethic and the free market mechanism.	81.6	71.9	80.6	75.5
A free society can exist under a capitalistic system.	77.3	70.8	73.4	75.1
Efficient management can only be achieved through capitalism.	57.4	47.9	53.9	53.1
Capitalists are entitled to the reward of profits because they assume the risk of loss.	78.3	65.6	72.3	75.9

CONCLUSION

Despite tumultuous business- and economy-related changes in the 1980s, the capitalism attitudes of the general public still remain positive. Males have become more skeptical of capitalism, whereas the attitudes of females have remained relatively constant. In 1989 age *per se* bore no relationship to capitalism attitudes, although an aging effect is now observable in the data. Attitudes toward capitalism remain significantly related to education. The more education an individual possesses, the more positive is the individual toward capitalism.

Even though general public attitudes toward capitalism appeared to have become slightly less positive, those of college students seem to have become somewhat more positive, both absolutely and relative to the general populace. Although this finding may initially seem counterintuitive, it may be due to a variety of reasons, including shifts in educational majors, changing collegiate lifestyles, and the fact that college students have generally been less directly affected by many of the events previously described.

NOTES

[1]See, for example, "American Japanophobia," *The Economist,* Vol. 313 (November 18, 1989): 15-16.

[2]Yoshi Tsurumi, "The Japanese Conspiracy: A New Hoax on the American Public," *Pacific Basin Quarterly*, Vol. 11 (Winter/Spring 1984): 3.

[3]Jeremy Main, "A Golden Age for Entrepreneurs," *Fortune*, Vol. 121 (February 12, 1990): 120-125.

[4]Due to changes in the level of household income from 1980 to 1989 and the smaller sample size in 1989, different income categories and a smaller number of categories were used in 1989 than in 1980.

[5]The average was computed as

$$\sum_{1}^{16} (\text{abs} [1989 \text{ agreement percentage} - 1980 \text{ agreement percentage}])$$

[6]Norval D. Glenn, *Cohort Analysis* (Beverly Hills, California: Sage Publications, 1977).

6

Conclusion

The objective of this book was to empirically document the public's understanding of, attitudes toward, and perceptions of capitalism. This chapter summarizes the research reported and discusses the implications of that research. It also discusses the need for continual monitoring of the public's views of capitalism through a social indicator approach.

UNDERSTANDING CAPITALISM

The evidence is clear regarding the public's understanding of and knowledge regarding capitalism. When asked to define capitalism, 27 percent of the general public was unable to provide any definition whatsoever. Of the individuals who were able to provide a definition, less than half, 47 percent, correctly defined capitalism. When these two numbers are considered simultaneously, the result is that only 35 percent of the general public is able to correctly define capitalism. As Figure 6.1 illustrates, this percentage is significantly less than the percentage of the general public able to define constructs often thought of as synonyms for capitalism—American enterprise, free enterprise, and private enterprise.

Not only does the general public lack an understanding of capitalism, it also has a misunderstanding of capitalism. Indeed, a slightly higher percentage of the general public (38 percent) defined it incorrectly than defined it correctly. One out of eight individuals surveyed defined capitalism in terms of a political system. Terms such as "restriction of rights/limited freedom" and "bureaucracy/excessive government" are examples of terms used by survey participants to define capitalism.

In Chapter 2 we stated that dictionary definitions and common literary definitions of capitalism are outmoded.[1] We subsequently offered a definition of capitalism that focused on it being a dynamic ideology and

Figure 6.1 The Public's Definitional Knowledge of Capitalism

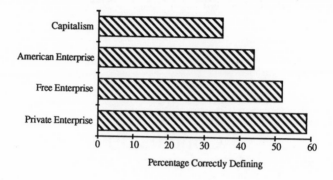

Percentage Correctly Defining

stressed its cultural associations and implications. While this definition is a useful starting point for discussion purposes, it is no doubt too sophisticated to succinctly convey to the American public.

A more straightforward definition of capitalism, yet one that conveys its multifaceted nature, is that of Bork. He defined capitalism as "not merely an economic system but a complex of institutions, attitudes, a culture."[2] Bork's definition served as one of the attitude items in the research.

In both the 1980 and 1989 general public studies, survey participants were asked to indicate their degree of agreement with Bork's definition. Table 6.1 summarizes the results obtained in the two studies. A substantial majority of the general public, 84 percent, agreed with Bork's definition in 1980. In 1989, although agreement had declined somewhat, more than three-quarters of the individuals interviewed still agreed with his definition. These percentages indicate strong agreement, both in an absolute sense and relative to capitalism-related topics investigated in our research and business-related research in general. Further, as the table reveals, the relationship between agreement with the definition and education is strongly monotonic in both surveys. The more education an individual possesses, the greater the likelihood the individual will agree with the statement. As will be discussed later, data such as these signal the need for additional research and the continual monitoring of the public's understanding of capitalism.

Surveys have consistently demonstrated that the public is "sadly deficient in its knowledge of basic business and economic facts of life."[3] Hence, the present findings are not an aberration. If it were deemed advisable to improve the public's understanding of capitalism, a long-term commitment of resources—financial and creative—would be required. Previous attempts to increase the public's economic literacy through increased education have typically failed.[4] Whether one agrees or disagrees with the basic tenets of capitalism, it is necessary to communicate its essfence in such a fashion that a rational public dialogue can occur. For

Table 6.1   "Capitalism is more than an economic system—it is a complex of institutions, attitudes, and cultures"

| | Percentage Agreement | |
Group	1980	1989
Total sample[*]	83.5	76.9
Gender[**]		
Male[*]	87.7	76.6
Female	79.0	77.2
Age[**]		
25-34	83.6	75.8
35-44	84.1	79.9
45-54	84.4	79.8
55-64	82.8	77.6
65 and over	78.9	72.3
Education[**],[***]		
Less than high school	71.5	67.7
High school	78.9	73.0
Some college	84.5	78.9
College graduate[*]	89.0	83.8

[*]1980-1989 difference statistically significant at p<.001 using a t-test.
[**]1980 difference(s) statistically significant at p<.001 using an F-test.
[***]1989 difference(s) statistically significant at p<.001 using an F-test.

this to happen will require a major effort that goes beyond the formal educational system.   What is required is what Bernstein terms "an affirmative ethic" that elicits the commitment of a strongly proactive constituency.[5]

TRENDS IN ATTITUDES AND PERCEPTIONS

Contrary to what one might believe from the media, the public generally has favorable attitudes toward, and perceptions of, capitalism. Especially when compared with its two major competitors—socialism and communism—capitalism is viewed positively by the American public. Moreover, despite the often virulent attacks on capitalism in the literature, the public appears to remain firmly disposed toward it.[6] Indeed, in the mid-1980s, several businessmen became media celebrities.[7]

However, it is important to note that (1) these attitudes and perceptions are moderated by demographic characteristics, and (2) the attitudes and perceptions are fluid and subject to change over time.

The benchmark study suggested that

- Males were more favorably disposed toward capitalism than were females.
- The 45-54 age group was more favorably disposed toward capitalism than was any other age group.
- The more education an individual possessed, the more positive were that individual's attitudes toward capitalism.

The follow-up study resulted in somewhat different findings. In 1989

- There were no significant differences between males and females in their attitudes toward capitalism.
- There were no significant attitudinal differences among age groups.
- The more education an individual possessed, the more favorable were that individual's attitudes toward capitalism.

The attitude findings are extremely intriguing and literally cry out for further research. For example, in the benchmark study, males were significantly more favorable toward capitalism than were females. A possible explanation for this finding is that attitudes toward capitalism may be related to employment or participation in the workforce. Hence, as more women entered the workforce in the 1980s, it was anticipated that female attitudes toward capitalism would become more positive and coincide with those of males. However, the 1989 study indicates that this did not happen. Female attitudes toward capitalism remained relatively stable. Male attitudes toward capitalism became significantly less positive and more in tune with those of females. The homogenization of attitudes is a topic that merits more focused attention in the future. The shift in male attitudes may be artifactual or substantive. It may be that males simply experienced a regression-toward-the-mean effect or reacted to economic or social conditions. However, given the widespread nature of the decline, this is probably unlikely; more likely is the existence of a societal shift occurring in attitudes toward capitalism.

Of the demographic characteristics investigated, education seems to possess the most consistent relationship with attitudes toward capitalism. Since there is a societal trend toward more education, this would imply attitudes will become more favorable as time progresses. However, although there was a strong monotonic relationship between capitalism attitudes and education, survey participants at all levels of education were less positively disposed toward capitalism in 1989 than they were in 1980. Hence, while the relationship is still maintained, attitudes became somewhat less positive.

The public's shift in attitude is best illustrated by the agreement percentages for the item "capitalism must be altered before any significant improvements in human welfare can be realized." As Table 6.2 shows, 38 percent of the survey participants agreed with this statement in 1980, whereas 52 percent did so in 1989. The difference is statistically and substantively significant, especially when one considers the fact that a slight majority of the participants agreed with this statement in 1989. The table reveals that whereas the overall sample evinced a shift of 14 percentage points, the shift was not uniform across demographic subgroups. Shifts larger than 14 percent were observed for males (22 percent shift), survey participants 25-34 (18 percent shift) and 45-54 (18 percent shift) years of age, and survey participants who did not graduate from high school (17 percent shift). Whether these shifts represent growing dissatisfaction with capitalism as a system or reflect current events remains to be seen.

A notable finding of the research is the public's positive view of "private enterprise." Of the three synonyms used for capitalism, private enterprise was correctly defined by the highest percentage of the public (59 percent). In general, private enterprise appears to evoke associations with small business. Two-thirds of the survey participants asked to define private enterprise used the phrase "one can own his own business" or something similar. This was a significantly higher percentage than that for capitalism (28 percent). A later study found that on a relative basis, ten times as many survey participants associated private enterprise with small business than associated capitalism with small business. Moreover, the public viewed small business as "mom and pop" operations—the smallest of the small. The message therefore is clear. Although they are not completely isomorphic, the term *private enterprise* should be used if favorable attitudes and associations need to be evoked because it appears to have a better connotation than capitalism.

In brief, the public does not seem to have a good grasp of capitalism, with a large percentage either not understanding or misunderstanding it. Even so, the public evaluates capitalism positively, in spite of the fact that perceptually it tends to be viewed more ambiguously than its synonyms.

FUTURE LEADERS

The attitudes of future societal leaders (college students) are an interesting counterpart to those of the general public. Analogous to the general public, college students are generally favorable toward capitalism in

Table 6.2   "Capitalism must be altered before any significant improvements in human welfare can be realized"

Group	Percentage Agreement	
	1980	1989
Total sample*	38.4	52.0
Gender**		
Male*	31.0	51.5
Female	47.1	52.5
Age**		
25-34*	38.3	56.3
35-44	42.3	50.8
45-54*	33.8	51.6
55-64	40.4	44.1
65 and over	44.8	53.3
Education***		
Less than high school*	49.8	67.2
High school	46.2	53.7
Some college*	39.7	52.5
College graduate*	32.4	44.0

*1980-1989 difference statistically significant at $p < .001$ using a t-test on mean scale values.
**1980 difference(s) statistically significant at $p < .001$ using an F-test.
***1989 difference(s) statistically significant at $p < .001$ using an F-test.

an absolute sense. On a relative basis, though, in 1980 college students were somewhat less positively disposed toward capitalism than was the general public. However, by 1989 the differences in attitudes were inconsequential. This is because of the general public becoming less positively disposed toward capitalism and the students becoming slightly more positively disposed. The latter is likely due in part to the changing composition of academic majors and lifestyle changes.

Two observations regarding college students' attitudes toward capitalism are particularly interesting. First, even though their attitudes in 1989 appeared to be similar to those of the general public, in comparison with general public survey participants who either attended college or were college graduates, their attitudes were less favorable toward capitalism. This suggests that education *per se* does not lead to more favorable attitudes toward capitalism. There are significant within-student attitude differences (e.g., students majoring in business vs. those majoring in liberal arts). Hence, perhaps something beyond college, such as work experience, influences attitudes toward capitalism.

Second, although single-item analyses are fraught with difficulties, it is instructive to view percentage agreement with the item, "Capitalists are entitled to the reward of profits because they assume the risk of loss." Table 6.3 suggests that

- In 1980 college students were significantly less in agreement with the item than were members of the general public who attended or graduated from college. By 1989, though, there were no substantive differences between these groups with respect to this item.
- The college student "cohort" displayed greater percentage agreement with the item in 1989 (76 percent) than it did in 1980 (66 percent).

MONITORING CHANGES

The country is at a historic moment in time. It is the beginning of the last decade of the twentieth century. Not only will a new century dawn in a few years, but indeed, a new millennium. Changes in the political and economic infrastructures of the world are taking place at an accelerating rate. During the last half of 1989, changes that virtually no one would have predicted six months, one year or ten years earlier occurred with such rapidity as to shake the very foundations of the world.

Given an apparent move toward worldwide acceptability of capitalism, there is a need to closely monitor the American public's understanding of, attitudes toward, and perceptions of capitalism on a timely basis. Perestroika notwithstanding, given the globalization of business, the world economy, and possibly "Fortress Europe," it is imperative that the public understand the basic tenets of capitalism so that an appropriate public sector/private sector dialogue can occur.

McClosky and Zaller, among others, believe the public's view of capitalism tends to swing back and forth like a pendulum.[8] They have noted that capitalism tended to be negatively viewed in the 1960s and 1970s, but that it was positively viewed in the early 1980s, a period coincident with our early surveys. It may well be that our 1989 survey of the general public captured the beginning of another pendulum swing. Whether this is true, or simply an aberration, is an empirical question that requires further research.

Table 6.3   "Capitalists are entitled to the reward of profits because they assume the risk of loss"

Group	Percentage Agreement	
	1980	1989
General public	78.3	72.3
College students	65.6	75.9
General public education		
Less than high school	54.3	58.1
High school	70.3	68.4
Some college	78.2	75.5
College graduate	85.0	78.6
General public age		
25-34	78.8	72.4
35-44	76.1	72.9
45-54	80.5	73.3
55-64	73.5	75.3
65 and over	75.5	68.1

In particular, there is a need for continuing research on the public's understanding of, attitudes toward, and perceptions regarding capitalism. Systematic, periodic surveys are necessary to monitor changes in the public's view of capitalism.

Indeed, it has been argued that a social indicator research paradigm should be used to construct a framework in which the state of capitalism as a social institution could be systematically assessed.[9] This framework would contain both longitudinal and cross-sectional components. It would build upon the research reported here and allow the systematic testing of numerous hypotheses about the public's view of capitalism. For example, on the basis of the present research, the possible interaction of education and age on attitudes toward and perceptions of capitalism over time merits investigation. Only when such analyses have been conducted will a sufficient data base be available from which to assess the existence, causes, consequences, and relative importance of secular trends and cyclical oscillations in the norms and expectancies of capitalism as an ideological institution in American society.

NOTES

[1]As an aside, there appears to be considerable agreement with this position. For instance, Robert C. Solomon, noted business philosopher, argues that both capitalism and its opponent terms should be confirmed to the same rubbish heap as "mercantilism" since they are "no longer terms that are of any descriptive use in understanding what we do and believe in" (personal communication, July 28, 1988).

[2]Robert H. Bork, "Will Capitalism Survive?" *Yale Alumni Magazine and Journal,* Vol. 61 (April 1978): 15-17.

[3]See, for example, "Are the Media to Blame?" *Editor and Publisher,* Vol. 117 (October 27, 1984): 9, and Edward L. Hennessy, Jr., "Business Ethics: Is It a Priority for Corporate America?" *FE: The Magazine for Financial Executives,* Vol. 2 (October 1986): 14-19.

[4]Karen F. A. Fox and Bobby J. Calder, "The Right Kind of Business Advocacy," *Business Horizons,* Vol 28 (January-February 1985): 7-11.

[5]Paul Bernstein, "Capitalism's Elusive Constituency," *Business Horizons,* Vol. 29 (November-December 1986): 2-8.

[6]Jack Cashill, "Capitalism's Hidden Heroes," *Fortune,* Vol. 111 (February 18, 1985): 159-161.

[7]"Business Celebrities," *Business Week,* No. 2952 (June 23, 1986): 100-104, 107ff.

[8]Herbert McClosky and John Zaller, *The American Ethos: Public Attitudes toward Capitalism and Democracy* (Cambridge, Massachusetts: Harvard University Press, 1984), Chapter 9.

[9]Kenneth C. Land, George Kozmetsky, and Robert A. Peterson, "Assessing the Current State of Capitalism: A Social Indicators Approach" (Austin, Texas: The IC^2 Institute, 1984).

Suggested Readings

Berger, Peter L., *The Capitalist Revolution: Fifty Propositions about Prosperity, Equality, and Liberty* (New York: Basic Books, 1986).

Halal, William E., *The New Capitalism* (New York: John Wiley & Sons, 1986).

Harrington, Michael, *The Twilight of Capitalism* (New York: Simon and Schuster, 1976).

Heilbroner, Robert L., *The Nature and Logic of Capitalism* (New York: N. W. Norton & Company, 1985).

Lipset, Seymour M., and William Schneider, *The Confidence Gap* (New York: The Free Press, 1983).

Magdoff, Harry, *The Deepening Crisis of U. S. Capitalism* (New York: Monthly Review Press, 1981).

McClosky, Herbert and John Zaller, *The American Ethos: Public Attitudes toward Capitalism and Democracy* (Cambridge, Massachusetts: Harvard University Press, 1984).

Redwood, John, *Popular Capitalism* (London: Routledge, 1988).

Schumpeter, Joseph A., *Capitalism, Socialism and Democracy* (New York: Harper & Brothers, 1942).

Index

About the Editors

ROBERT A. PETERSON holds the John T. Stuart III Centennial Chair in Business at The University of Texas at Austin and is the Charles Hurwitz Fellow at the IC² Institute at The University of Texas at Austin. He has published more than 150 books and articles and is a former editor of *The Journal of Marketing Research.*

GERALD ALBAUM is Professor of Marketing at the University of Oregon and Senior Research Fellow at the IC² Institute.

GEORGE KOZMETSKY is Executive Associate for Economic Affairs, The University of Texas System, and Director of the IC² Institute at The University of Texas at Austin. He is a co-founder of Teledyne and a Fellow of the American Association for the Advancement of Science.